PRAISE FOR TH

"As an executive search professional and small business owner, I have interviewed thousands of "C" level executives over a 30-year career. I've enjoyed many conversations with that cohort about the importance of investing in the physical and mental well-being of their employees – their greatest asset. 'The Ageless Executive' is a well-researched, compelling read that reaffirms the importance of that investment. A highly recommended and timely book."

Kerryn Wilson, Director & Founder, Wilson Research

"This book is a powerful testament to the critical connection between well-being and performance. 'The Ageless Executive' offers actionable insights and practical strategies to empower anyone to unlock their true potential and thrive in today's world and its demanding business landscape."

Paul Middleton, Naturopath & Personal Trainer

"In The Ageless Executive, Edua presents powerful insights as to how you can unlock the secrets of peak performance. The tools and resources detailed in each chapter are easy to understand and Edua gives practical tips about how to find out what can really work for you as you navigate the corporate environment without having to suffer from stress and burnout."

Michael Fullick, author of The Strategic Advisor

"As an entrepreneur, I've always believed that our greatest asset is our people. 'The Ageless Executive' is a compelling guide that reaffirms the importance of investing in the physical and mental well-being of employees. It's an eye-opener for anyone looking to build not just a successful business but also a vibrant and resilient organizational culture."

Savvas Leondas, Director, Savvas Leondas Enterprises Pty Ltd

"I've spent over 25 years dealing with "C" Level Executives in my role and have witnessed firsthand the significant demands and challenges faced by these individuals daily. The ability to do more with less continues to be a major factor in most executives lives and while there are many resources available to assist in managing work, the focus on managing physical and mental health is not as heavily supported. The Ageless Executive is a compelling guide that reaffirms the importance of investing in the physical and mental wellbeing for those working in high stress roles providing insights, both traditional and more alternative, allowing for peak performance and happiness."

Garry Medland, Director – Executive Search

THE AGELESS EXECUTIVE

GLOBAL
PUBLISHING
G R O U P

Global Publishing Group
Australia • New Zealand • Singapore • America • London

THE
AGELESS
EXECUTIVE

The Science of Longevity in the Boardroom

EDUA POTOR

DISCLAIMER

The information presented in this book is based on the opinions and research of the author and is provided solely for informational and educational purposes. If you decide to apply the material in this book to yourself, the authors and publishers assume no responsibility for your actions, decisions, or any resulting consequences. The content of this book is not intended to substitute a one-on-one relationship with a qualified healthcare professional, and it should not be considered medical advice. It is intended to share knowledge, information about health and opinions based on the research and experiences of the authors and their collaborators. Readers are encouraged to consult with a qualified healthcare professional for personalized advice and treatment.

First Edition 2023

National Library of Australia
Cataloguing-in-Publication entry:

The Ageless Executive: The Science of Longevity in the Boardroom - Edua Potor
1st ed.
ISBN: 978-1-925370-80-5 (pbk.)

A catalogue record for this book is available from the National Library of Australia

Published by Global Publishing Group
PO Box 258, Banyo, QLD 4014 Australia
Email admin@globalpublishinggroup.com.au

Proudly printed in Australia

Cover and book design by NGirl Design

For further information about orders:
Phone: +61 7 3267 0747

This book is dedicated to the visionary CEOs, the relentless entrepreneurs and the astute decision-makers who understand that true success goes beyond financial gains. It is dedicated to those who believe that the well-being of themselves and their employees is paramount, transcending the boundaries of traditional profit-focused metrics.

To the executives who have realized that investing in health and wellness is not just a luxury but a necessity, this book is for you. It is a testament to your commitment to building organizations that prioritize the holistic well-being of every stakeholder. Your dedication to fostering a culture of vitality and resilience has the power to transform lives, fuel exceptional performance, cultivate meaningful relationships and elevate your brand.
In the pages of "The Ageless Executive" you will find a comprehensive compendium, meticulously crafted to empower you with the knowledge and tools necessary to achieve and maintain peak performance. May this manuscript serve as your guide, enabling you to tap into the best available information, keeping your brain health vibrant and fortifying your body and mind with the strength you need to excel in today's fast-paced and demanding business world.

As you immerse yourself in these insights, may you discover the pathways to personal well-being and unleash your true potential. May this book serve as a source of inspiration and practical wisdom, equipping you with the strategies to overcome challenges, embrace change and cultivate a thriving ecosystem within your organization(s).

I extend my deepest gratitude to all the scientists, writers, researchers, health pioneers and executives who have shared their experiences, knowledge and wisdom, shaping the foundation of this work. Your invaluable contributions have illuminated the path for others, and your commitment to promoting health and wellness is an inspiration to us all.
Finally, I dedicate this book to my family, friends and loved ones who have supported me throughout this journey. Your unwavering encouragement and belief in my vision have been my guiding light. With heartfelt appreciation I thank you for standing by me, empowering me to embark on this endeavour and encouraging me to make a difference in the lives of executives around the world.

May "The Ageless Executive" be a catalyst for positive change, leading us towards a future where health and well-being are at the forefront of every decision-maker's agenda.
With profound gratitude,

ACKNOWLEDGEMENTS

Acknowledgements for some inspiration derived from these notable figures who have contributed to the understanding of health, brain health, rejuvenation and longevity in the past 30 years.

Aubrey de Grey - Biomedical gerontologist known for his research on rejuvenation therapies and extending human lifespan.

Bruce Lipton - Cellular biologist and author known for his research on epigenetics and the impact of beliefs and perceptions on health and well-being.

Daniel Amen - Psychiatrist and author known for his research on brain imaging and the impact of lifestyle interventions on brain health.

David Perlmutter - Neurologist and author known for his work on the gut-brain connection and the role of diet in brain health, author of "Grain Brain."

David A. Sinclair - Professor and researcher specializing in ageing and longevity, known for his work on the role of sirtuins and NAD+ in cellular health.

David Wolfe - American author – promoting raw foodism, detoxification and alternative medicine. Creator of the "Longevity Now Program".

Deepak Chopra - Physician, author, and alternative medicine advocate, known for his work on mind-body healing and holistic approaches to health.

Elizabeth Blackburn - Molecular biologist and Nobel laureate recognized for her research on telomeres and their role in ageing and disease.

Michael Pollan - Author and journalist known for his exploration of food and agriculture, including the book "In Defense of Food" and "The Omnivore's Dilemma."

Robert Lustig - Pediatric endocrinologist and author known for his research on the impact of sugar and fructose on health, author of "Fat Chance."

Steven R. Gundry - Cardiothoracic surgeon and researcher focused on the impact of diet and gut health on ageing and longevity.

Valter Longo - Biogerontologist and expert in fasting and calorie restriction, known for his research on the effects of fasting on health and longevity.

Dean Ornish - Physician and researcher known for his work on lifestyle medicine and reversing heart disease through diet and lifestyle changes.

Mark Hyman - Physician and author advocating for functional medicine and addressing the root causes of chronic illness.

Michael Greger - Physician and author known for his work on plant-based nutrition and the impact of diet on health and longevity, author of "How Not to Die."

Terry Wahls - Physician and researcher who reversed her own multiple sclerosis symptoms through a nutrient-dense diet, author of "The Wahls Protocol."

Get Hundreds of Dollars' Worth of FREE Bonuses

Get a Free 30 minutes one-on-one consultation with me, valued at $497!

Fast and effective "Ageless Executive in-Power" session, where we will look at where you are now, where you want to be and what are the next best steps.

Access your session by sending me an email with the subject "Book - Bonus Coaching" at edua@theagelesexecutive.com

AND

Download four e-books with an accumulated total of 200 pages of priceless information, expanding on some of the subjects covered in this book.

ALKALIZE And Get Younger

Learn the Keys for Rejuvenation

Intermittent Fasting Protocol

Repair your cells, enhance your brain function, and lose weight

PERFECT DETOX

The Power of Internal Body Cleaning

The Ultimate Detox Guide to Optimize Your Performance and Well-being in 7 days

SUPERFOODS IN YOUR KITCHEN

For Health and Longevity

Go to:

https://theagelessexecutive.com/resources

OR

Scan the following QR Code to access your Bonuses

CONTENTS

CHAPTER ONE

Hydration - Foundation to Life

"*Water in nature is naturally structured even though you can't see any form in it. At a molecular level, under a microscope, water has shapes that are organized in geometric patterns. Spring water, waterfalls and glaciers are structured. And the water in fruits and vegetables is naturally structured.*

If we want to get our bodies into alignment with nature and health, we need to be thinking about hydration with structured water."

Dr. Gerald Pollack

CHAPTER ONE

Hydration - Foundation to Life

Water is our most precious resource and the fate of humans and water is inextricably linked.

Pure water is absolutely the foundation of health and deep cellular nourishment.

You can literally live a better life through better hydration. Not only will water sustain your life, but the right kind of water will give you energy, reduce your high blood pressure and even reverse your ageing process!

The quality of water is more important than the quantity of water. Spring water is one of the purest sources of hydration and usually still contains an electrical charge, produced by the motion of its journey from mountain to spring.

Every cell and every function of your body needs pure water and your brain cannot function optimally if you are dehydrated.

The information in this chapter is possibly the most significant if you want to upgrade your body and your mind for superior performance!

Benefits of Hydration to Improve Your Productivity and Rejuvenate Your Brain

Water's extensive capability to dissolve a variety of molecules has earned its title of "universal solvent" and it is this talent that makes water such an invaluable life-sustaining force. On a biological level, water's function as a solvent helps cells transport and use substances like oxygen or nutrients.

Hydration is an essential part of your daily routine because water doesn't just hydrate your body, it also regulates temperature, transports nutrients and oxygen throughout the body and removes waste products from cells. It also helps with cognition, mood and focus. It boosts your energy levels and keeps you alert during the day which in turn will help you be more productive.

It can also help with weight management, reduce muscle cramps but most importantly rejuvenate your brain and, with cellular hydration through osmosis, repair your DNA and trigger a reverse ageing process.

The human body is composed of two thirds water, essential for all bodily functions, providing intracellular and intercellular hydration.

Virtually all symptoms of ageing are the result of cellular dehydration accompanied by free radical damage.

The water content of an infant is 70%, an adult 60% and an elderly person's water composition is down to 50/55%! Hydration and rejuvenation are directly connected!

Every single part of the body holds water and the hydration content distributed throughout the body varies between the brain with 85% water content, down to the teeth with 8-10% water content!

Body's water content			
Eyes	95%	Kidneys	83%
Blood	94%	Heart	75%
Lungs	85%	Muscles	75%
Brain	83%	Teeth	8%

Water has the biggest role inside your body as it flushes out waste, cools the body, assists the flow of blood through the circulatory system, decreases fatigue, supports brain function and gives your skin that healthy glow!

Dehydration Can Lead to Many Chronic Conditions [1]

Hydration ought to be used by the scientific community as a key barometer for our health, as it was demonstrated in 1992 by Dr. Fereydoon Batmanghelidj in his book "Your Body's Many Cries for Water". [2]

Batmanghelidj asserts that chronic dehydration is the root cause of many ailments and explains the damaging effects of dehydration. He discusses the role of water in the body and his belief that water can transform the health needs of society. However, he was considered controversial with his proposals related to the treatment of diseases and conditions with water.

Batmanghelidj believed that a dry mouth is not the first symptom of thirst but one of the last. He suggested that in fact, as people age, their ability to recognize thirst decreases. This means they drink less and age even faster. Based on his research, he claimed that water can protect people from several conditions. His book is cited by many nutritionist/physicians.

Today it is common knowledge that dehydration is at the root of many diseases, that ageing is a function of cellular water loss and that 50% to 75% of people are chronically dehydrated.

The most powerful, transformative, life-giving force on the planet is water.

Peter Schenk

Water Alkalinity and The Health of Your Blood [3-4-5-6]

The pH of water is measured on a scale from 0 to 14, with 7 being neutral. Anything below 7 is considered acidic and anything above 7 is considered alkaline.

Live blood analysis, when viewed on a LCD screen microscope, will show that with healthy blood, red blood cells are well separated, repelling each other due to their negative charge. In an alkaline state, blood will circulate faster throughout the arteries and hence supply more oxygen to the body and get the body into a reverse ageing state.

The Extraordinary Properties of Natural Water [7]

Viktor Schauberger (1885-1958) was a pioneering Austrian revolutionary naturalist who pointed the way to a completely new understanding of the vast potential of natural energy. He studied fish in streams and closely observed the natural water cycle.

Most importantly, his observation of nature made him conclude that there is something very special about how water naturally spirals downwards with gravity. This phenomenon is found in waterfalls, in creeks and rivers.

The vortex is the key to creating the energetic disturbances of liquid crystal water. "Life is movement and is epitomised by water, which is in a constant state of motion and transformation, both externally and internally. As the fundamental basis of all life, water is itself a living entity and should be treated as such".

Movement Is an Expression of Energy and Energy Is Synonymous with Life. Flowing Water Transports Energy

Chlorination of water, while planned to eliminate the danger of water-borne infections, destroys a wide range of microscopic organisms, both valuable and destructive. Even more significantly, it cleans the blood (which is 80% water) and thusly, kills numerous safe immune-enhancing micro-organisms.

Water behaves differently from other liquids; it reaches its greatest density at +4.0C, when it expands and changes its quality. The highest state of density is its highest health, energy content and life-force.

Conceived in the coolness of virgin forests, water gathers trace elements and minerals on its upward way to emerge as a spring. Here it begins its long-life-giving cycle as a sparkling, lively, translucent stream, bubbling, gurgling, whirling and gyrating whilst naturally self-cooling, spiralling, convoluting and maintaining its vital inner-energies, health and purity.

Flowing water transports all the necessary minerals, trace elements and other subtle energies.

The faster the water flows, the greater its carrying capacity of purification ability and the more it deepens its riverbeds. This is due to the formation of in-winding, longitudinal, clockwise/anti-clockwise alternating spiral vortices down the central axis of the current which constantly cools and re-cools the water, maintaining it at a healthy temperature and leading to a faster, smoother, spiral flow. Ultimately the spring becomes a river and has the capacity to protect its deeper water strata from the centre of the water mass and in this way reducing the danger of flooding.

Vortexing Action of Water

The spiral, vortical motion is what led Viktor Schauberger to the formation of his theories about "implosion", creating the conditions where the germination of harmful bacteria is inhibited, and the water remains disease-free.

"The forest is the habitat of water and as such the habitat of life processes too, whose quality declines as the organic development of the forest is disturbed." [8]

We must plant trees for our very lives and care for the very limited stocks of water still available. Protect water from sunlight, allow the water to breathe for it to stay alive and healthy. Storing vessels for water are best made in natural stone, timber, and terracotta. Best shapes to maintain life would be eggs or elongated egg-shapes, as these produce the optimal results.

Historically, it is evident that earlier civilizations such as the Egyptians and Greeks stored their grains and liquids in terracotta amphorae, sealed with beeswax. Efficacy of the properties of such vessels was proven when grains of wheat have been found that were still viable after storage over 2,000 years and grew when planted!

Viktor's theories were tested at the Stuttgart University of Technology, in West Germany, in 1952 by Professor Dr. Ing. Franz Popel. The tests showed that when water is allowed to flow in its naturally ordained manner, it generates certain energies, ultimately achieving a condition called "negative friction".

"The Upholder of the Cycles which supports the whole of Life, is WATER. In every drop of water dwells the Godhead, Life, the Soul of primal substance. Water itself is a living entity, sustainer of all life."

Viktor Schauberger

The vortexing action of water causes implosion in the water which restores the natural structure, health, and vitality of water, it also micro-clusters the water molecules and increases and activates dissolved oxygen in the water.

Viktor Schauberger was quite ahead of his time with his observations and theories and quite aligned with the more recent discovery of Dr. Gerald H Pollack. [9-10-11]

New Frontiers of Water Science! [12-13-14]

In 1998 with the help of the first human magnetic resonance imaging, nuclear magnetic resonance (NMR spectroscopy, a research technique to determine the magnetic properties of the substances atomic nuclei), the 4th phase of water was first identified and represented a discovery of major proportions.

Water does not exist in single unit molecules but forms a molecular population (cluster). A regular tap water cluster holds 15-20 molecules, which makes it very hard for the body to absorb, whereas an Ionized water cluster, or structured water, holds 3 to 5 molecules.

Water is then absorbed much more readily by the body – it is said to be more bio-available. The smaller micro clusters can more easily pass through cell membranes.

The Fourth Phase of Water [15] **Water Isn't What You Think It Is:**

An important property of alkaline water is micro clustering. Ionization breaks up these clusters into smaller groups called micro clusters.

Alkaline water has smaller molecules than other types of water, a higher pH and these tiny clusters permeate through cell walls faster, resulting in quicker hydration and easy solubility.

Structured water is not new; it has always been present in nature and in all of us, but we now can see it with NMR as a distinct phase of water, used to renew and to charge itself.

That renewal and charging state is called structured water or the fourth phase of water.

That fourth phase of water is when water releases the spark of life into all living things.

It was discovered in the University of Washington by Dr. Gerald H Pollack, water scientist and professor of Biomedical engineering. It was whilst using nuclear magnetic resonance spectroscopy, most known as NMR, that Dr. Pollack made his discovery.

Structured water is also referred to as organized water, hexagonal water and liquid crystalline water. Liquid crystals are a unique phase of matter.

These 6-sided crystal formations look and behave like living cells: these cells vibrate at a frequency 40,000 times faster than normal water.

Like solid crystals, the repeating pattern provides an efficient pathway for the smooth flow of energetic information.

Liquid crystals store and transmit information just like solid crystals, yet they are flexible and many times more responsive. More about this in the next paragraph.

**Water is life's matter and matrix, mother and medium.
There is no life without water.**

Nobel prize winner, Albert Szenbt-Görgyi

Hydration Delivers Information [16]

Hydration isn't just wet; it is coherent wave signals that deliver information in the form of electrical signals from cell to cell.

Here's a good place to say that structured water research is still so new that it flies under many names: structured water, fourth phase of water, ordered water, liquid crystalline, exclusion zone or EZ, even H3O2. This water can store light and transmit energetic information and information is frequency!

EZ – The Exclusion Zone [17]

When touching most surfaces, water transforms itself into so-called EZ (Exclusion Zone) water, also known as structured water or fourth phase water. EZ water, whose formula is H3O2, differs dramatically from H2O.

2017 was a breakthrough year as respected universities from FOUR major water research teams (Oxford, University of California at Berkeley, University of Stockholm and Cornell) published articles on new states of water.

Structured water is found in nature – it is the water in streams and springs, in fruits and vegetables, and in our cells. It was recently "identified" as structured water with the molecular structure of H3O2.

H3O2 is 10% denser and has more oxygen than standard H2O. The most amazing distinction is that while H2O has no charge, organized water does have an electrical charge. This is how water creates a battery which delivers and stores energy inside us. This is the fuel required to move, think, recuperate and repair. H3O2 is nature's water.

Hypotheses that EZ water is important for cellular energy production and biological function have been explored by several researchers. (18-19-20)

How To Build EZ In Your Cells [21]

Here are six (6) ways to increase EZ water in our body and charge up your cells.

- Water: Raw material for building EZ
- Green Juicing: plant-cell water contains EZ
- Turmeric, Coconut water: builds EZ
- Sunshine: Light builds EZ
- Sauna: Infrared Light builds EZ
- Grounding: Negative charge builds EZ

Earth is vast repository of negative charge and the human body is positively charged so bare-foot walking will recharge our battery. (Much more on this in later chapter)

Structured Water Hydrates Better Than Regular Water

H302	H20
Electrical charge	No charge
Intracellular water – hydration	Extracellular water – dehydration
Efficient detoxification	Limited detoxification
Charged molecules give energy	No charge, lifeless
Physics is the science, goal is energy	Chemistry is the science, goal is purity
"Alive" – aligned with nature	"Dead" – corrupted by man-made influences
Living/ mature water – giver	Juvenile water – taker
Easy to drink	Hard to drink

Drink a Better Kind of Water [22]

Structured water will better hydrate, reduce fatigue, improve focus, reduce stiffness, deliver longevity, improve skin, hair, eyesight, mood – in short, get your own juices flowing! When you drink a better kind of water you can reduce your volume liquid intake and still be optimally hydrated because it is a different stage of water that moistens longer and conducts electrical functions in the body far more efficiently. This gel like water can seem as thin as a liquid but is slightly silkier and it can also expand to become as thick as gelatine.

Water has the power to heal.

Water is the most programmable material on the planet.

Turn to nature for optimal hydration and drink water from springs and streams. You can also hydrate with natural juices, smoothies and water rich vegetables, the smartest strategy designed by nature.

Water From Fresh Food Can Be Up To Two Thirds More Hydrating Than Water From a Glass

The best strategy to reach the highest level of hydration is to get hydration from water AND food.

Fruits and vegetables are made up of structured water and hence are more hydrating and more nutritious.

The gel water in fruits and vegetables is structured by nature, packed with nutrients and fibres so it doesn't just flash flood through but gets absorbed by the cells more readily.

Fruits and vegetables contain 80/98% gel water and are packed with antioxidants and proteins with their amino acids and vitamins. Fruits and vegetables also carry minerals like calcium, magnesium, potassium and sodium. Fresh fruits and vegetables offer optimum hydration for our bodies, minds and moods.

Gina Bria, anthropologist, was researching indigenous tribes from desert regions around the world to understand how they survived drought conditions. In her research she discovered that desert dwellers found their water in plants to hydrate themselves.

Smoothies are also an excellent way to hydrate as they blend fruits or vegetables with their plant fibres, helping us to remain hydrated longer and benefiting from cellulose which sweeps clean micro-sized toxins, cellular waste and debris that are constantly coming into our bodies from our environments.

Charge Your Water With Energy!

The easiest way to charge water is to add a pinch of salt such as Himalayan Pink Salt or Celtic Grey Mineral Sea Salt.

They contain sodium, potassium, and other trace minerals. Sodium provides positively charged ions while potassium provides negatively charged ions. This combination generates electrical charges and transmits impulses to the cell membranes and keeps them functioning optimally.

You can also squeeze lemon into your water, as it has incredible cleansing and mucus-dissolving properties.

Eat/Drink Fruit and Vegetables with High Water Content [23]

List of vegetables high in structured water (H3O2)	List of Fruits high in structured water (H3O2)
Asparagus – Up to 93% water	Apples 84%
Bok Choy (Pak Choi) – Up to 95% water	Blueberries – 85%
Broccoli – 90.7%	Cantaloupe – 90.2%
Cabbage – Up to 93% water	Grapefruit – 90.5%
Carrots – 90%	Grapes – 81.5%
Cauliflower – 92.1%	Kiwi – 84.2%
Celery – 95.4%	Pears – 84%
Cucumbers – 96.7%	Pineapple – 87%
Green Bell Peppers – Up to 94% water	Raspberries – 87%
Lettuce – Up to 96% water	Starfruit – 91.4%
Okra – Up to 93% water	Strawberries – 91%
Peppers – 93.9%	Watermelon – 91.4%
Portabella Mushrooms – Up to 93% water	
Radishes – 95.3%	
Romaine Lettuce – 95.6%	
Spinach – Up to 92% water	
Sprouts – 86.5%	
Swiss Chard– Up to 93% water	
Tomatoes– Up to 95% water	
Watercress– Up to 95% water	
Zucchini – 95%	

You can also create structured water from tap or bottled water with a vortexing device which imitates water flowing down a mountain stream.

Structured water = healthy cells [24]

Water is arguably the most important substance in the Universe and without its remarkable ability to dissolve substances and transport vital information to every cell in our body, we could not exist.

Information is frequency.

More recent studies by Dr. Gerald H Pollack and Dr. Mae-Wan Ho have also confirmed the water substance within all living cells is primarily structured water, and its accompanying negative charge seems to be critical for proper cell function.

To highlight this point, Dr. Pollack explained, "Healthy cells are negatively charged and in the range -60 to -95 Millivolts (mV) whereas cancer cells are positively charged and in the range of -30 to – 20mV". [25]

Change the water around your cells and change your life!

Today, it is common knowledge that dehydration is at the root of many diseases, that ageing is a function of cellular water loss and that 50% to 75% of people are chronically dehydrated.

So, drinking structured water will reverse dehydration and bring about many benefits including increasing the possibility for longevity.

Instant absorption and Improved bodily functions

Cells absorb structured water instantly with a more efficient ingestion of nutrients, better excretion of toxins resulting in improved cellular activity and bodily functions.

It is the quickest way to restore optimal pH balance.

> # The most powerful, transformative, life-giving force on the planet is water.
>
> ## *Peter Schenk*

Best Anti-Ageing Secret: Drink Alkaline Water, Structured Water and Get Healthier and Younger!

"Wai" in Hawaiian means fresh water, the kind of water that is necessary to sustain life, water for the growing of crops and sustenance for man and beast. It also means wealth.

In the Hawaiian pantheon, the god Kane is particularly distinguished, for he is the father of living creatures. An ancient Hawaiian mele (chant) speaks to the cultural and spiritual importance of water. It is timeless. [26]

Hydration And Consciousness

Masaru Emoto was a Japanese author and pseudoscientist who said that human consciousness influences the molecular structure of water. [27]

Emoto's conjecture evolved over the years, and his early work revolved around pseudoscientific hypotheses that water could react to positive thoughts and words and that polluted water could be cleaned through prayer and positive visualization. [28]

Dr. Emoto's work, described in his book "Messages from Water", is a study of the effects of human consciousness on the molecular structure of water. His book contains stunning before and after photographs of water molecules transformed into beautiful water crystals by intention, words, prayer, and meditation, demonstrating the connection of water to our consciousness. [29]

If our thoughts can do this to the water, and we are made of 60-80% water, how can our thoughts and intentions impact on others and what can their thoughts do to us?

Hydration And Vibration

The universe is composed of vibration.

Dr. Len Horowitz - Harvard-trained award-winning investigator, reviewed the science of electro genetics and proved that broadcasting the right frequency can heal the DNA. He helped to develop OxySilver with NASA scientists to keep astronauts healthy. Oxysilver contains energetically structured water made with the 528Hz frequency to be especially absorptive and vibrationally acceptable to the human body. [30]

In his book, "DNA: Pirates of the Sacred Spiral", Dr. Len H. reviewed the science of electro genetics that speaks to humanity's fundamental spirituality when combined with this mineral water and 528Hz frequency. He says that this combination has the power to heal every physical malady. [31]

Likewise, his book: " Walk on Water", talks about the mathematics, music and physical mechanics of hydro-creationism science, where he proves that, by broadcasting the right frequency, the broadcasting can help open your heart to peace and hasten healing.

In Dr Len Horowitz's words:

"We now know the love signal, 528 Hertz, among the six core creative frequencies of the universe, the geometry of physical reality, universally reflects this music; the third note, frequency 528, relates to the note MI on the scale and derives from the phrase "MI-ra gestorum" in Latin meaning "miracle.""

528Hz is the exact frequency used by genetic biochemists to repair broken DNA!

The "solfeggio frequencies" are a set of musical pitches which originate in centuries-old Gregorian chant and come from a numerological manipulation of decimal representations of frequencies in cycles per second, or Hertz. [32]

These findings have been independently derived, peer reviewed, and empirically validated.

UT -- 396 Hz -- Negative Field Release
RE -- 417 Hz -- Allowing & Creating Change
MI -- 528 Hz -- Transformation and Miracles (DNA Repair)
FA -- 639 Hz -- Love & unity
SOL -- 741 Hz -- Intuition & Enlightenment
LA -- 852 Hz -- Spiritual Sight/Awareness

A molecule of water is like a tetrahedron of water molecules – Merkabah in its geometric shape nodes- is like a bio-holographic projection of divinity before it manifests in the quantum field of consciousness!

Water is the most sacred fluid on this planet, the creative juice of the Universe. If we give love and thanks and projects these as frequencies and sounds to water, we can solve all health issues, heal our DNA, and supercharge our cells for superior performance.
[33- 34- 35]

> **If you want to find the secrets of the universe, think in terms of energy, frequency and vibration. Our entire biological system, the brain, and the Earth itself, work on the same frequencies.**
>
> *Nikola Tesla*

Hydration And Movement

Research has found that the fascia transports water molecules through the body and physical activity promotes this process. Get your arms up over your head, once a day, to help flush your armpit lymph nodes and keep channels clear and move toxins out, as part of the hydration cycle.

According to Gina Bria, anthropologist and hydration researcher, "twisting movements are especially good for hydration."

Any movement, any squeezing or twisting of your tissues generates electricity, making your hydration have more charge, become more conductive and more efficient.

Spending even a little time doing yoga or stretching helps your body to stay hydrated. [36]

Little movements throughout your day makes a BIG effect. There is a study that cites that people who fidget decrease mortality by 30%!

So, keep moving and keep hydrating to stay healthy, alert and vibrant!

SUMMARY OF CHAPTER ONE
Hydration - Foundation to Life

- Benefits of Hydration to improve your productivity and rejuvenate your brain
- Dehydration can lead to many chronic conditions
- Water alkalinity and the health of your blood
- The Extraordinary Properties of Natural Water
- Movement is an expression of energy and energy is synonymous with life. Flowing water transports Energy
- Vortexing Action of Water
- New frontiers of Water Science
- The fourth Phase of Water
- Hydration delivers information
- EZ- The Exclusion Zone
- How to build EZ in your cells
- Structured Water Hydrates Better Than Regular Water
- Drink a better kind of water
- Water from fresh food can be up to two thirds more hydrating than water from a glass
- Charge your water with energy!
- Eat/Drink fruit and vegetables with high water content
- Structured water = healthy cells
- Best Anti-Ageing secret: Drink Alkaline Water, structured water and Get Healthier and Younger!
- Hydration and Consciousness
- Hydration and Vibration
- Hydration and Movement

CHAPTER TWO

Nutrition and Rejuvenation

"Don't eat anything your great-grandmother wouldn't recognize as food. There are a great many food-like items in the supermarket your ancestors wouldn't recognize as food (Go-Gurt? Breakfast-cereal bars? Non-dairy creamer? Stay away from these."

Michael Pollan

CHAPTER TWO

Nutrition and Rejuvenation

A brief History of Nutrition

Once upon a time all we ate was life-sustaining food. Food was our unconditional friend but in one generation it has become a suspect with the potential to thicken our arteries, weaken our immune system and contaminate our bodies! When we prepared a meal, we didn't focus on precise recipe measurements and had not heard of Glycaemic index.

The industrial food supply was reformulated in the 1970s and gave us advice about low fat or fat free foods. The irony is that both Australia and America got really fat on this new low-fat diet with high occurrence of obesity and diabetes when fats were replaced by carbohydrates. (Fat doesn't make you fat but carbs do). Many foods with "low fat" labels had a high sugar content, to make that food more palatable and food became designed to deceive our senses.

In the 1980s "food" was replaced by "nutrients": eggs or breakfast cereal or fruits were replaced by "fibre" and "cholesterol" and "saturated fat" .

Instead of food, we now have nutrients with the scientific promise, that if you eat more of the right ones and less of the bad ones, you will live healthier and avoid chronic diseases.

There is also the birth of a new dietary language with terms like polyunsaturated, cholesterol, monounsaturated, carbohydrate, fibre, polyphenols, amino acids and carotenes.

So much information! So many choices! We are offered edible food-like substances with health claims by the latest study.

This has led us to so much nutritional confusion and anxiety.

For eaters, what happened to health and happiness? Unless you have become a successful Breatharian, the aim of this chapter is to arm you with useful information with a clear advice: always choose fresh over processed or over-refined!

Nutrition And the Average Western Diet

The average Western diet is one of the worst diets in the world. It consists of high amounts of meat, dairy, sugars and saturated fats which can lead to a variety of health issues.

The liquids ingested are often sugary drinks or alcohol and large quantities of caffeine. The average Western diet indicates that the 150 pounds of sugar ingested by the average person annually is the equivalent of 22 teaspoons of sugar a day. One can of Coke contains up to 10 teaspoons of sugar, which means that one coke a day contains the equivalent of 30 pounds of sugar a year! This means that 32 glasses of neutral pH water are needed to balance one glass of Cola! It also means that it creates an ideal ACIDIC environment for your body which can cause inflammation and other health problems and even cancer! Whilst there are many factors that can contribute to the development of cancer, one of the most important is sugar consumption. Studies have shown that consuming too much sugar can lead to an increase in insulin levels, which in turn can feed cancer cells.

Nutrition plays an important role in maintaining a healthy lifestyle and it is essential to understand what foods are beneficial for our bodies.

Have you ever looked at the ingredients list on a food label and been confused by all the different names for sugar? It's no wonder, as there are over 60 different names for sugar that can be found in food products. From agave nectar to xylitol, it can be hard to keep track of them all. Here is a list of the top 50 for you to be aware of.

List of 50 names behind which sugar hides

Agave nectar	Confectioner's sugar	Florida crystals	HFCS (high fructose corn syrup)	Panocha
Barbados sugar	Corn syrup	Fructose	Honey	Raw sugar
Barley malt	Corn syrup solids	Fruit juice	Icing sugar	Refiner's syrup
Beet sugar	Date sugar	Fruit juice concentrate	Lactose	Rice syrup
Brown sugar	Dehydrated cane juice	Galactose	Malt sugar	Sorbitol
Buttered sugar	Demerara sugar	Glucose	Maltodextrin	Sorghum syrup
Cane juice	Dextran	Glucose solids	Maltose	Sucrose
Cane sugar	Diastatic malt	Golden sugar	Mannitol	Treacle
Carob syrup	Diatase	Golden syrup	Maple syrup	Turbinado sugar
Castor sugar	Ethyl maltol	Grape sugar	Molasses	Xylitol

A Sip of Soda: How Soft Drink Impacts Your Health [1]

- Twenty minutes after drinking a soda your blood sugar spikes, causing an insulin burst. Your liver responds to this by turning any sugar into fat.

- Forty minutes later, caffeine absorption is complete. Your pupils dilate, your blood pressure rises; as a response, your liver dumps more sugar into your bloodstream. The adenosine receptors in your brain are now blocked, preventing drowsiness.

- 45 minutes later, your body ups your dopamine production, stimulating the pleasure centres or your brain.

- This is the same effect that heroin would have on your body!

How Do Addictive Foods Affect the Brain?

Most of the food available on the market today contains one or more of the five ingredients - fat, sugar, salt, caffeine and wheat. These ingredients are highly addictive and can be found in almost all processed foods. While these ingredients are necessary for taste, texture and flavour of food products, they can have detrimental effects on our health when consumed in excess.

Excessive consumption of these ingredients can lead to addiction as they stimulate the reward centres in our brain and they present the strongest addictive and influencing factors in our diets.

Ashley Gearhardt, PhD - University of Michigan, is the co-creator of Yale University's Food Addiction Scale, which places many of today's processed foods in the same category as drugs of abuse. She suggests signs of addiction, aside from irresistible craving for certain foods, are their capacity to interfere with moods and behaviours just like substance dependence. [2]

Nutrition Awareness

If you are used to consuming sugar and caffeine on a regular basis then you may experience significant withdrawal symptoms when you remove them from your diet. This is because both sugar and caffeine can be addictive substances and your body has become accustomed to their presence. As a result, when they are removed from your diet, your body will go through a period of adjustment as it adapts to the new reality. During this period of adjustment you may experience headaches, fatigue, irritability, difficulty concentrating and other withdrawal symptoms.

However, it is possible to make the switch to a healthier lifestyle and manage, reduce or eliminate any withdrawal symptoms as they arise.

Become a detective with your food and be aware that fructose and corn syrup are sugars and do refer to the above table if you are uncertain of what a listed food item is.

Know that the first three items listed on a food label are the highest content of that substance in that food.

The Secret of Food Barcodes / Labels

The best way to protect yourself from pesticides, rodenticides or fungicides is to eat only organically grown food.

Since that is not always available, be aware of the stickers on your produce, so that you can make better choices.

Food Barcodes

Food Barcodes from Best to Worse		
5 digit - starting with 9	9 - XXXX	= Organic
5 digit - starting with 8	8 - XXXX	= MO - GE
4 digit – conventionally grown	XXXX	= Contains pesticides

Detox and Heavy Metals Detox

Our bodies are amazing at filtering and getting rid of unwanted substances, but it is still important to be mindful of what we put into our bodies. Ingesting toxins can have serious consequences on our health, so it is best to avoid them as much as possible.

So, the first rule is to AVOID toxins and the second rule is that if you have ingested some, make sure you ELIMINATE them as much as possible.

Your liver is a filter for many toxins, but heavy metals isolate themselves in specific organs or tissues.

"Fish and shellfish concentrate mercury in their bodies, often in the form of methylmercury, a highly toxic organic compound" according to the "Better Health Channel" within the Department of Health of the State Government of Victoria.

General symptoms of heavy metal toxicity are diarrhea, nausea, abdominal pain, vomiting, shortness of breath, tingling in your hands and feet, chills, weakness, brain fog.

Mercury is the most found heavy metal toxin.

Many of us still have dental amalgam (fillings) with mercury and are having or had vaccines, most of which include mercury.

You can help your body to remove heavy metals and escort them out safely.

Firstly, avoid eating large fish (Tuna) and bottom feeders such as shrimps and prawns.

Get your dentist to remove mercury amalgams.

Be aware that mercury can cause DNA damage.[3]

Heavy Metal Smoothie Detox

Heavy metals can be removed from the body by the daily use of chlorella, wheatgrass and spirulina.

Cilantro herb or Coriander, taken daily, can help remove mercury from brain tissue. Simply add these ingredients to your daily smoothie and you can also enhance the taste with raw cacao which also has a high antioxidant content.

You may need a reminder that the human body is composed of more than two thirds water.

Scientific research has shown that the right hydration can repair the DNA and in reverse, when the cells become dehydrated it can create DNA damage.

Since mercury can cause DNA damage and the right hydration can repair DNA, to help detoxify – simply drink more water!

Best and Worst Foods - Organic Versus Conventional

Most pesticide contaminated produce – (EWG-Environmental Working Group) [4]	
Strawberries	Exposed to multiple noxious chemicals and fumigants – Contain 60X more pesticide application by weight than corn - Average of 8 varieties of pesticides which are linked to cancer and reproductive damage and banned in Europe
Spinach	Holds the highest pesticide residues by weight – Linked to ADHD and various neurological impairments in children due to permethrin, a neurotoxin insecticide banned in Europe – DDT still used by some growers
Kale	Contaminated with the herbicide DCPA (Dacthal), which has been banned in Europe since 2009 because of cancer risk
Peaches	Can contain up to 56 pesticides and fungicides with main one Fludioxonil and neonicotinoids which are harming wildlife as well as human health and may cause acute respiratory, cardiovascular, and neurological symptoms to oxidative genetic damage and birth defects
Pears	Found at least 5 different pesticides can be used with Pyrimethanil, a fungicide and Phenyl phenol known carcinogen and hormone disruptor
Nectarines	Detected 33 pesticide residues with known carcinogens, hormone disruptors and reproductive toxins. Also toxic to honeybees, our most important pollinators
Apples	Only 4 pesticide residues were found. However, after harvest, they are bathed in Diphenylamine to keep their skin pretty while in cold storage. European officials have banned this chemical; may contribute to stomach and oesophagus cancer
Grapes	Loaded with pesticide residues including 8 cancer causers and often treated with 19 pesticides that are toxic to honeybees Nonorganic raisins contain residues from two or more pesticides

Peppers - Capsicum	Most types of pesticides detected! 115 in total! Two of the most found pesticides: Acephate and Chlorpyrifos which can cause nervous system problems
Cherries	About 50% cherries sampled contained residues of Bifenthrin, a neurotoxin that kills insects by paralysis and is moderately harmful to mammals (including humans) added to 42 other chemical residues found should cause concern
Blueberries	Out of range of 17 different pesticides, two to be aware of: Phosmet, and Malathion banned in Europe. Still approved for US greenhouse usage
Green Beans	Main pesticide used: Acephate found to be 500 times the allowed limit! Also included: Chlorothalonil and both Carbendazim and Bifenthrin, banned in EU and classified as potential carcinogens
Least Pesticide Contaminated – Mostly Clean	
Avocados	The single pesticide found on avocados, Imiprothrin, appears benign in toxicity studies
Sweet Corn	Steer clear of bioengineered corn but other than that, any corn, fresh, or frozen, organic or not seems to be pesticide free
Pineapple	The most common chemical is Triadimefon, but their thick skins seem to create an effective barrier, so that it is fine to eat
Onions	Even though a large range of pesticides is used, they are removed as you peel the onion, rendering it safe for consumption
Papayas	Some are bio-engineered, but mostly contain very few pesticide residues
Sweet Peas (Frozen)	Out of 76 pesticides found in frozen peas, only one, Dimethoate appears in more than 4% samples. Quite safe to eat
Asparagus	Only a few pesticide residues found and if you wash your asparagus in water containing baking soda, it will get rid of any of the last minor residues

Honeydew Melon	Largely pesticide free! Also, just like other thick-skinned fruit and vegetable, it is unlikely the edible flesh part of the fruit would have any pesticides
Kiwifruit	Known to have residues of the fungicide Fludioxonil, which may have hormone-disrupting effects. But if you don't eat the skin of the kiwi, you'll likely be fine
Cabbage	Only Methomyl and Flonicamid are known to be associated with health issues. And they appear in max.1.3% of tested samples
Mushrooms	The most common pesticide used on mushrooms, Thiabendazole, is a pharmaceutical prescribed for humans to treat pinworm and hookworm infections. Not considered harmful
Mangoes	Out of 11 pesticides, most are found in less than 1% of samples, with most common: Thiabendazole . Overall rated ": very good"
Sweet Potatoes	Out of 19 different pesticides, the most prominent Dicloran, is a pre- and postharvest fungicide used to prevent soft rot. Peel your sweet potatoes to remove any residue
Watermelons	Around 10 different pesticides used on watermelons are harmful to bees and other pollinators, which are essential for watermelons to grow. But some farmers are beginning to reduce pesticides used on and near watermelon fields to save pollinators and improve yields. Most pesticides were only found in less than 1% of watermelon samples and only found on the outer rind of the fruit, not the flesh
Carrots	34 different pesticide residues were found in less than 1% of samples. The most common was Linuron, which is sprayed on newly emerging carrot plants, but still came up with an "excellent" rating

How About Real Food?

It is hard to be a whole food clone. You can't put oat bran in a banana, whereas you can put oat bran into nearly every processed food.

There are so many reasons why eating real food is the best way to support your health and achieve and retain optimal life performance!

What real foods offer:

- Low in sugar: even fruit containing sugar is a much healthier option and offers naturally structured water and fibre
- Fantastic for your skin! Think avocado and chocolate
- Lower triglycerides and high in healthy fats
- So much variety, hundreds of choices
- Cheaper in the long run and helps you keep healthy
- May reduce disease risk, as suggested by large body of global research
- Excellent for gut health as many real foods function as prebiotics
- Higher level of natural satiation would prevent overeating
- Supportive to dental health because they contain less refined sugars and carbs and many real foods promote teeth and gum health
- Better for the environment: real food based on sustainable agriculture is good for the planet
- Packed with antioxidants and nutrients
    - Please compare the number of nutrients in any packaged food containing more than 5 items with the chemical composition of any common food plant which is so much more complex
    - Out of all the amazing components that have been identified in garden-variety thyme, if we only considered the antioxidants category, you would see this huge list of beneficial molecules:

4-Terpineol, alanine, anethole, apigenin, ascorbic acid, beta carotene, caffeic acid, camphene, carvacrol, chlorogenic acid, chrysoeriol, eriodyctiol, eugenol, ferulic acid, gallic acid, gamma-terpinene isochlorogenic acid, isoeugenol, isothymonin, kaempferol, labiatic acid, lauric acid, linalyl acetate, luteolin, methionine, myrcene, myristic acid, naringenin, oleanolic acid, p-coumaric acid, p-hydroxy-benzoic acid, palmitic acid, rosmarinic acid, selenium, tannin, thymol, tryptophan, ursolic acid, vanillic acid

- o   It is hard to compete with nature!

Acid and Alkaline – What Does It Have To Do With Ageing?
Acid and Ageing

When the pH level of your internal fluids is low, it can have a significant impact on your digestive system. This is because the acidity of your body's fluids affects how well your digestive system functions. Low pH levels can lead to indigestion, bloating and other digestive issues. It can also make it harder for your body to absorb nutrients from food, leading to deficiencies in essential vitamins and minerals. This can potentially cause serious damage to your health.

Most degenerative diseases attributed to ageing have been scientifically linked to mineral deficiencies that result in your body fluids becoming more acidic. This includes cancer, osteoporosis and heart disease and other diseases such as allergies, gallstones and kidney stones.

Of course, you know by now that cancer thrives in an acid medium but cannot survive in an alkaline medium?

Acid also coagulates blood and blood has major problems flowing around fatty acids which is when capillaries clog up and die.

The skin also suffers and when deprived of life-giving healthy blood, loses elasticity, and begins to wrinkle. Even with a face lift or liposuction, the acid remains and continues its relentless advance.

Without a basic acid/alkaline balancing plan, every part of your body works ever harder to maintain health - because every system (all the organs, the lungs, even the skin) is involved in the maintenance of correct blood pH.

In 1933 Dr. William Howard Hay published "A New Health Era". He maintained that all disease is caused by autotoxication (or "self-poisoning") due to acid accumulation in the body!

In later years, Dr. Theodore A. Baroody author of "Alkalize or Die", says essentially the same thing:

"The countless names of illnesses do not really matter. What does matter is that they all come from the same root cause ... too much tissue acid waste in the body!"

Alkaline Foods and Youthing

ALKALINE food lifestyle is the most powerful strategy you can use to OPTIMIZE your health, boost your body with ENDLESS energy, MELT AWAY excess pounds and get younger!

It is easy to reverse the pH levels in your body.

Nutrition Ideal – 80% Alkaline Foods

Choose a balanced diet which contains 80% alkaline foods with an allowance of 20% Acidic foods.

Keeping this ratio will encourage your body to get younger!

Dr. Robert Young when interviewed on CNN stated that Alkaline foods are the Fountain of Youth!

Practical Tips:

Healthy Cell Regeneration Can Be Promoted Through The Following Foods:

- Raw seeds, nuts, and grains
- Fruits (prunes, raisins, blueberries, strawberries, cherries, blackberries, raspberries)
- Vegetables (broccoli, spinach, beets, peppers, sprouts)
- Bean and lentils
- Seaweed (hormone thyroxin – nervous system)
- Barley greens
- Antioxidants (Vit C & E)
- Olive and evening primrose oil (joints, skin)
- Foods containing omega-3 fatty acids

For Maximum Health and Longevity:

Eat food. Not too much. Mostly plants

The Acid Alkaline Chart

80% Alkaline / 20% Acid						
Most Alkaline	Alkaline	Least Alkaline	Food Category	Least Acid	Acid	Most Acid
Stevia	Maple syrup, Brown Rice syrup	Raw honey, raw sugar	SWEETENERS	Processed Honey, Molasses, Barley Malt Syrup, Maple Syrup	White Sugar, Brown Sugar, Fructose	NutraSweet, Equal, Aspartame, Sweet 'N Low
Lemons, Watermelon, Limes, Grapefruit, Mangoes, Papayas, Cantaloupe	Dates, Figs, Melons, Grapes, Papaya, Kiwi, Gooseberry, Blueberries, Raspberry Strawberry, Apples, Pears, Raisins, Currants, Passionfruit	Oranges, Bananas, Cherries, Berries, Pineapple, Peaches, Apricot, Nectarine, Coconut, Avocados	FRUITS	Plums, Prunes, Processed Fruit Juices	Sour Cherries, Rhubarb	Blackberries, Cranberries,
	Almonds	Chestnuts	NUTS / SEEDS	Pumpkin Seeds, Sunflower Seeds, Brazil nuts, Pecan, Macademia, Pistachio	Pecans, Cashews, Walnuts	Peanuts
Asparagus, Endives Vegetable Juices, Parsley, Broccoli, Raw spinach, Broccoli, Watercress,	Okra, Squash, Celery, Onions, Green Beans, Lettuce, Herbs Beets, Garlic Zucchini, Pumpkin Sweet Potato, Carob, Alfalfa sprouts, Peas	Carrots, Tomatoes, Fresh Corn, Mushrooms, Cabbage, Okra Cucumber, Leeks Eggp plant, Radish Brussel sprouts.- Cauliflower, Soybeans, Peas, Tofu, Bell-Pepper Potato skins, Olives, artichoke	BEANS VEGETABLES LEGUMES	Cooked Spinach, Kidney Beans, String Beans, Lentils	Potatoes (skinless) Pinto Beans, Navy Beans, Lima Beans Chocolate	
Olive oil	Flax Seed Oil	Canola Oil	OILS	Corn oil		
Kudzu Roots	Umeboshi Plum	Sea Salt vegetable Ginger, Tamari Apple Cider vinegar, Miso Spices	CONDIMENTS	Nutmeg, Mustard	Ketchup Soy Sauce	Pickles Jams, jellies
		Amaranth, Millet, Wild Rice, Quinoa, Essene Bread, Sesame Seeds, Sprouted grains	GRAINS CEREALS	Sprouted Wheat Bread, Spelt, Brown Rice	White Rice, Corn, Buckwheat, Oats, Rye, Wheatgerm	Wheat, White Flour, Pastries, Pasta, Crackers, Refined Cereals, Pastries, Cakes
	Breast milk	Soy Cheese, Soy Milk, Goat Milk, Goat Cheese, Whey, Tempeh, Tofu	MEATS EGGS / DAIRY/ Replacements	Fish, Eggs, Butter, Raw cream, Yogurt, Buttermilk, Cottage Cheese	Turkey, Chicken, Lamb Raw Milk,	Pork, Cheese, Homogenized Milk, Ice Cream, Sweet Yoghurt
Herb Teas, Lemon Water	Green Tea	Ginger Tea	Herb Teas, Lemon Water	Tea	Coffee Chocolate	Beer, Soft Drinks, Wine, Liquor

www.TheAgelessExecutive.com

The Longevity Diet by Professor Valter Longo

In his book "The Longevity Diet", Dr. Longo suggests that 8 simple dietary changes could help us to live longer and healthier lives.

He proposes that a diet that is mostly plant-based with a pescatarian exception and smaller portions, supplemented with a multivitamin and mineral pill, plus an omega-3 soft gel, would be sufficient for excellent health.

He also advises to eat within a 12-hour window with your last meal 3 to 4 hours before sleep. He has created a "fasting-mimicking diet", which restrains calories, with a food intake of around 1000 calories/day for 5 days, three times year. He observed that this is sufficient to receive the same benefits of fasting, without going to a traditional no food/fasting. This low calory-state tricks the body in thinking that it is fasting and produces the same benefits of breaking down (killing) of damaged cells, replacing them and regenerating the body.

Since so many scientists are suggesting plant-based diets, you may be concerned about getting enough protein. You will be surprised to know that some plants have a higher protein content than some animal-based foods.

Where Do You Get Your Protein?

Top 10 sources of vegetable protein [5]

Spinach	49% protein	Kale	45% protein
Broccoli	45% protein	Mushroom	38% protein
Cauliflower	40% protein	Parsley	34% protein
Cucumber	24% protein	Green Pepper	22% protein
Cabbage	22% protein	Tomatoes	18% protein

Top 3 source of animal protein

Beef	25.8% protein
Chicken	23% protein
Eggs	12% protein

Protein per 100 gr serving from highest to lowest [6]	
Parmesan	36 g
Hemp seeds	32 g
Chicken breast	31 g
Halibut Fish	30 g
Turkey Breast	29 g
Peanuts	26 g
Shrimp	24 g
Part-skim mozzarella	24 g
Black Beans	22 g
	22 g
Ground beef	20 g
Pistachio	20 g
Salmon	19 g
Canned tuna	19 g
Tempeh	19 g
Pumpkin seeds	19 g
Oats	17 g
Eggs (2x)	12 g
Low-sodium cottage cheese	12 g
Edamame	12 g
Greek yogurt	10 g
Lentils	9 g
Chickpeas	8 g
Quinoa	4.5 g

The Ten Commandments

- Generally, eliminate anything that is white (sugar, fat, salt, pasta, flour) replace with Stevia / agave/ Himalayan salt/ Buckwheat

- Cut out coffee and spirits - replace with green tea and 1 glass red

- Don't be perfect, just be consistent, aim to feel happy

- Keep it simple = if grown in a garden, good for you - If made in lab, takes a lab to digest

- Have a good relationship with your food

- Less acid, more alkaline – 80-20 rule

- Avoid food ingredients that are a) unfamiliar, b) unpronounceable c) more than five in number or high in sugar

- Less stress - learn meditation

- Visualise being healthier and younger

- Food and Drink – Choose what will give you life force/chi and have fun with it

SUMMARY OF CHAPTER TWO
Nutrition and Rejuvenation

- A Brief History of Nutrition
- Nutrition and the average western diet
- Table – List of 50 names behind which sugar hides
- A sip of cola: The relationship of cola and cocaine
- How do addictive foods affect the brain?
- Nutrition Awareness
- The secret about food barcodes/ labels
- Detox and Heavy Metal Detox
- Heavy metal smoothie detox
- Best and Worst foods – Organic versus conventional
- How about real food?
- Acid and Alkaline – what does it have to do with ageing?
- Acid and Ageing
- Alkaline foods and youthing.
- Nutrition ideal - 80% Alkaline Foods
- Alkaline and Acid magic chart
- Practical Tips for cell regeneration
- The Longevity Diet by Dr. Valter Longo
- Where do you get your protein? Top 10 sources
- List of protein from highest to lowest
- The 10 Commandments

CHAPTER THREE

Telomeres and Anti-Ageing

"You are in control of your aging through healthy habits. Telomeres listen to you, they listen to your behaviours, they listen to your state of mind,"

Elizabeth Blackburn,

President of the Salk Institute for Biological Studies

The Nobel Prize in Physiology or Medicine 2009

CHAPTER THREE

Telomeres and Anti-ageing

When I conducted my initial research on reverse ageing, I searched for foods and products supporting cell rejuvenation. I came across a range of super herbs and discovered a particular supplement incorporating these with a combination of multi-vitamins, promising reverse-ageing. I was convinced that I found the modern equivalent of secret ingredients, such as the famed mystical Hunza Valley stories of humans living extraordinarily long lives! Finally, I thought my quest was over and this could be my chance to touch immortality! I wanted to push the boundaries of beliefs and expand the realm of possibilities. I followed the trail down the rabbit hole to the original manufacturer and supplements formulation specialist, which in turn led me to a science laboratory/manufacturer in Reno, USA. This is how I learned about the discovery of telomerase which revolutionized longevity science and thrilled anti-ageing devotees. I am delighted to write about my discovery of telomerase and the crucial impact of telomeres, how they affect your ageing and energy loss and how to reverse these so that you can regain and retain peak performance at any age, in all areas of your life, from the boardroom to the bedroom.

Anti-Ageing and Telomeres and The Man Who Would Stop Time

This is probably one of the most impactful discoveries of the decade regarding reverse-ageing! Dr. Bill Andrews, one of the world's

leading scientists in the field of telomere biology has been involved in biotech research for 29 years and specifically researched the role of telomeres in cellular ageing. His company has been issued 37 US Patents some which are related to the extensive discoveries linked to "telomerase", the enzyme that activates telomere growth.

Telomerase is a relatively new science since February 2011.[1]

Dr. Bill has been pushing the limit of what we thought was possible to stop the ageing process by lengthening telomeres.

What Are Telomeres? Much More Than a Biology Recap

When I first encountered this information, I felt like I had to go back to the basics of biology. By understanding the fundamentals of genetics and molecular biology, I was able to gain a better insight into how this information could affect us and thus appreciate the full impact of this discovery.

- Telomere – from ancient Greek: Telos = end and Meros = part
- A human being is made of 100 trillion cells
- Every cell contains a nucleus and inside the nucleus are the Chromosomes – this is where the genes are
- A Chromosome is made up of 2 arms
- Each arm contains a single molecule of DNA coiled along the arm and goes from one end of each arm to the other end
- Telomeres are the caps at the end of each strand of DNA and these "caps" protect our chromosomes

DNA replication is an essential process for the survival of all living organisms. During this process, each time a cell replicates itself, it loses some of its telomere length. It is not a "wear and tear", but it is about the inability for a cell to replicate the end of the telomere as it shortens.

Over time, this would lead to cellular ageing and death.

Because telomere length is a biomarker of ageing, it is represented as a measurement of base pairs, or basis.

- Each telomere is about 15,000 basis long when we are conceived

- Telomeres start shortening at birth!

- As we go through life, our cells keep dividing and our telomeres get shorter
When telomere's length gets down to 5,000 basis long it represents a state of old age and it is at this level of measure that a human body dies of old age.

Simply summarised: telomeres shorten as we age and if we could lengthen them, we would reverse the ageing process.

Researchers Believe They Have Identified the Upper Limit of Human Mortality: 150 Years Old.[2]
How Come We Don't All Live to Be Centenarians?
How Can We Reverse Our Present Trajectory of Ageing?

Anti-ageing is a hot topic in the medical field, and telomeres are at the heart of it.

Dr. Bill Andrews, with his research and discovery, has presented possibilities to slow down or even reverse the effects of ageing. This would lead to longer lifespans, improved quality of life and help us better understand diseases such as cancer, Alzheimer's and Parkinson's which are all linked to cellular ageing. The exciting aspect of Dr. Andrews' discovery is that opportunities are endless when it comes to controlling the ageing process at a cellular level.

The Research About Telomeres and Telomerase Has Unlocked Some of The Secrets of Longevity And Improvement of Our Overall Health In Ways That Were Previously Unimaginable

In the last two generations we have seen tremendous progress in almost every field; we are able to enjoy a higher quality of life than our predecessors and generally we are living longer.

This progress has been made possible for a variety a cumulative reason such as:

- Better sewage systems
- Refrigeration
- Cleaner water
- Antibiotics
- Blood pressure medicine
- Coronary artery by-pass surgery
- Cholesterol medications
- Chemo and Radiation Therapy
- Exercise trends
- Better diets
- Better care of our teeth
- Antioxidants
- Anti-smoking campaigns
- Vaccines
- A.G.E. breakers
- Hormone replacement
- Caloric restriction
- Resveratrol

Whilst many of these areas have substantially benefitted us, I would question some of them as they can be replaced with more natural choices and yield either better results or not cause any side-effects.

Changing telomeres timelines can be simple. For example, we can accelerate the shortening by being overweight and smoking or decelerate the shortening with lifestyle choices: Healthy food – Antioxidant or meditation for example. First, let's have a look at the culprits of age acceleration.

The Main Accelerators of Ageing
THE BIG 3 – Inflammation – Glycation – Methylation

Inflammation and ageing

Many age-related diseases are associated with chronic Inflammation as does poor physical function when the body becomes the target for disease. [3, 4, 5]

Low-grade inflammation promotes a vicious cycle of oxidative stress, telomere dysfunction and cell senescence that accelerates the ageing process.

Elevated omega-6 has been linked to inflammatory diseases such as [6]

- Cardiovascular disease
- Type 2 diabetes
- Obesity
- Metabolic syndrome
- Irritable bowel syndrome & inflammatory bowel disease
- Macular degeneration
- Rheumatoid arthritis

- Asthma
- Cancer
- Psychiatric disorders
- Autoimmune diseases

The evidence of negative impact from omega-6 is overwhelming!

Moreover, a 2018 study found an association between a higher dietary intake of omega-6 fats and inflammation that caused tissue damage and disease, hence the greatest risk of death from heart disease. [7]

The Arthritis Foundation say that omega-6 fatty acids may trigger the body's production of pro-inflammatory substances, potentially worsening symptoms in people with arthritis. [8]

Other research from NCBI, has linked diets high in omega-6 fats to obesity. [9]

Omega-6 fats belong to a group of unsaturated fats known as polyunsaturated fatty acids (PUFAs).

Watch out for these top inflammatory food ingredients and avoid them as much as possible:

- **Sugar:** The American Journal of Clinical Nutrition warns that processed sugars trigger the release of inflammatory messengers called cytokines, and look out for many names ending in "ose", such as fructose or sucrose

- **Saturated Fats:** these trigger adipose inflammation, an indicator for heart disease and aggravates arthritis inflammation. These come in the form of Pizza, Cheese, full-fat dairy products, meats, pasta dishes and grain-based desserts [10]

- **Trans Fats:** Harvard School of Public Health researchers found trans fats trigger systemic inflammation. Trans fats are found in fast foods and other fried products, processed snack foods, frozen breakfast products, cookies/biscuits, donuts, and crackers. Check ingredient labels for partially hydrogenated oils!

- **Omega-6 fatty acids** are found in oils such corn, safflower, sunflower, grapeseed, soy, peanut and vegetable; mayonnaise; and many salad dressings. Omega-6 fats are common in processed foods like biscuits or crackers, in most fast food and all fried foods as also mentioned in the category of refined carbohydrates [11]

- **Refined Carbohydrates:** White flour products (breads, rolls, crackers) white rice, white potatoes (instant mashed potatoes, or French fries) and many cereals are refined carbohydrates. According to Scientific American, processed carbohydrates are high-glycaemic index foods which fuel the production of advanced glycation end (AGE) products that stimulate inflammation

- **MSG:** Mono-sodium glutamate (MSG) flavouring most Asian foods and soy sauce. These can be added to fast foods, prepared soups and soup mixes, salad dressings and deli meats, triggering inflammation and affecting the health of your liver

- **Gluten and Casein** in wheat, barley and rye, or casein, found in dairy products. Those with joint pain and small intestine challenges may find relief when adopting a gluten-free diet

- **Aspartame:** an intense artificial sweetener found in more than 4,000 products worldwide. Even though it is approved by the FDA, if you are sensitive to this chemical, your immune system may react to the "foreign substance" by attacking the chemical, which in return, will trigger an inflammatory response

- **Alcohol** if ingested in excess, can weaken liver function and cause inflammation. It is best eliminated or used in moderation

---

Research seems to suggest that early humans consumed equal amounts of omega-6 and omega-3 fatty acids in their diets and that this was beneficial to their health. A ratio of 1:1.[12]

However, nowadays, in a typical Western diet, the ratio of omega-6 to omega-3 fats is at least 20-to-1 ![13]

The Solution to Reduce Inflammation Naturally

The importance of redressing the balance between omega-6 and omega-3 is made evident by a study of Yup'ik Eskimos in Alaska, who on average consume 20 times more omega-3 fats from fish than people in the other 48 states! This suggests that a high intake of these fats helps prevent obesity-related chronic diseases such as diabetes and heart disease. [14]

The balance can be easily restored by eating healthy phytonutrients–omega-3s [15]

Several clinical studies have shown that decreasing the n-6:n-3 ratio protects against chronic degenerative diseases. One study showed a huge difference that when replacing corn oil with olive oil and canola oil to reach an n-6:n-3 ratio of 4:1 led to a 70% decrease in total mortality! [16-17]

Among vegetable oils and foods, only flaxseed oil had the ideal 4 to1 Antioxidants ratio.

Oil	Omega-6 Content	Omega-3 Content	
Safflower	75%	0%	
Sunflower	65%	0%	
Corn	54%	0%	**Omega-3s**
Cotton Seed	50%	0%	**are**
Sesame	42%	0%	
Peanut	32%	0%	**your**
Soybean	51%	7%	
Canola	20%	9%	**3 amigos!**
Walnut	52%	10%	
Flaxseed	14%	57%	
Fish	0%	100%	

Eat an anti-inflammation diet [18]

You can slow down your telomere loss by fixing your omega-3 to omega-6 Ratio

The easiest way to fix your ratio of omegas is to eat 3 to 6 grams of omega-3 per day.

The more omega-3 fat you eat, the less omega-6 will be available to the tissues to produce inflammation. As covered above, omega-6 is pro-inflammatory, while omega-3 is neutral, so very simply put, a diet with more ʊ 6 and less ʊ 3 will increase inflammation. A diet of a lot of ʊ 3 and not much ʊ 6 will reduce inflammation.

Be mindful that Big Pharma provides over the counter and prescriptions of NSAIDs (ibuprofen, aspirin, etc..) to reduce the formation of inflammatory compounds derived from ʊ 6 fatty acids.

Would it not be much simpler to make an adjustment with your diet?

Glycation: The Issue and The Solution

What is glycation and why/how does it accelerate ageing?

Glycation is a process in which sugar and protein molecules combine to form glycated tissue, resulting in the formation of AGEs (Aged Glycation End-products), producing large numbers of damaging free radicals.

This process can lead to the development of tough and inflexible tissues, with external manifestations such as wrinkling of the skin. Indeed, as we age, our bodies become less able to break down these AGEs, resulting in an accumulation that further contributes to degradation of important body tissues and other signs of ageing.

Refined sugars are often seen as a major cause of a variety of health issues, including obesity, diabetes, heart disease and more. But as mentioned, these sugars can also speed up the ageing process and damage your skin cells, leading to wrinkles and age spots, while also damaging your organs and causing serious diseases. So, if you want to stay young and healthy for longer it's important to reduce or eliminate refined sugars from your diet. Not only will this help keep you looking and feeling younger for longer, but it will also help prevent serious health issues in the future.

Methylation: The Issue and The Solution

Methylation is an essential process for almost all your body's systems. It is a biochemical process that helps to regulate gene expression, DNA repair and the production of hormones and neurotransmitters. Without methylation our bodies would not be able to function properly. It is also important for maintaining healthy levels of inflammation in the body, which can help reduce the risk of chronic diseases such as cancer and heart disease. Methylation also plays a role in detoxification, energy production and immune system regulation. Methylation also affects sleep and your ability to handle stress.

Therefore, it is essential to ensure that your body has adequate levels of methylation to maintain optimal health.

> **Good news: you can control the deceleration of ageing!**

Fortunately, there are now easy solutions available to help manage methylation more effectively. These solutions include dietary supplements, lifestyle changes and other natural remedies that can help support healthy methylation levels. With the right approach it is possible to maintain optimal methylation levels for better overall health and wellbeing.

Leafy greens, folic acid, B6/magnesium, zinc, onions and garlic are all important components of managing methylation. These foods provide essential vitamins and minerals that help to keep our bodies functioning properly. Eating these foods regularly can help to reduce the risk of certain diseases and illnesses. They can also help to improve overall energy levels, mental clarity and getting the nutrients your body needs for optimal health and longevity.

Connection Between Ageing, Short Telomeres and Cancer

Whilst ageing is a natural process that affects all living organisms, it is associated with several changes in the body, including the

shortening of telomeres. Telomeres as previously mentioned are the protective caps at the end of chromosomes that help to maintain their stability and integrity.

Research also shows that high consumption (more than three servings per day) of ultra-processed foods had the greatest increased risk of shortened telomeres by 82 percent! [19]

As we age, our telomeres become shorter, and this can potentially lead to an increased risk of cancer. [20]

Telomeres are essential to preserve the integrity of the genome. Critically short telomeres lead to replicative cell senescence and chromosomal instability and may thereby increase cancer risk. [21]

WHAT TO DO?

The rate of telomere shortening can be either increased or decreased by specific lifestyle factors. Better choice of diet and activities has great potential to reduce the rate of telomere shortening or at least prevent excessive telomere attrition, leading to delayed onset of age-associated diseases and increased lifespan. [22]

The Most Important Thing You Can Do Is to Change Your Diet

- **EAT ORGANIC**
- Take supplements: antioxidants, VitC, VitE, VitB12, fish oil, L-glutathione (NAC), carnosine, CoQ10, N-acetyl-L-cysteine and DL-alpha lipoic acid: amino acids which are the building block of proteins
- **Glutathione**: Sulphur rich: broccoli, kale, cabbage, cauliflower, watercress, whey protein
- **Carnosine:** fish, milk, eggs, cheese

- **Organic vs Conventional:** Whenever you can, choose organic. Check out how Kirlian Photography demonstrated the differences between life force energies of organic versus conventional produce

- Conventional crops have 48% higher concentration of pesticide of cadmium (Also present in cigarettes)

- Organic foods have higher number of antioxidants with 69% higher flavanones.

The British Journal of Nutrition has published the research of Dr. Jessica Shade and Carlo Leifert highlighting both differences between organic/non-organic meat and the importance of food production and sustainability. [23]

The BIG 4 To Slow Down Telomere Reduction

1-Diet [24]

Eating a healthy diet is one of the best ways to reduce inflammation in the body and thereby reducing telomere shortening. This type of diet focuses on eating foods that are rich in antioxidants, omega-3 fatty acids and other nutrients that can help reduce inflammation. It also involves avoiding processed foods, refined sugars and trans fats which can increase inflammation.

Oxidative stress is caused by an imbalance between free radicals and antioxidants in the body and it can lead to a variety of health problems. The best way to reduce oxidative stress in your body is to eat a diet rich in antioxidants such as fruits and vegetables and taking specific supplements such as antioxidants, fish oil, glutathione (NAC), carnosine and CoQ10.

2-Exercise

Any exercise is always good and offers a well-established overall physical and mental benefit. Maximising the benefits of exercise with high intensity interval training (HIIT) is a form of exercise that involves short bursts of intense activity followed by periods of rest. It has become increasingly popular in recent years due to its effectiveness in burning calories and improving overall fitness.

Several studies have shown that HIIT lasting 1 to 4 mins interspersed with intervals of rest or active recovery, is superior to continuous moderate-intensity exercise and improves cardiorespiratory fitness, endothelial function and its markers, insulin sensitivity and arterial stiffness in hypertension! [25]

Scientific research printed in the Journal of Basic Research in Medical Sciences shows that HIIT can alter telomerase activity and telomere length. [26]

3-Sleep

So underestimated – if you don't sleep enough, your body gets inflamed and releases non global inflammatory cells in your body.

If you don't sleep, your body behaves just like you have an infection – It gets inflamed and your cells become a target for infection.

4-Meditation

The ends of linear chromosomes have attracted serious scientific study—and Nobel Prizes—since the early 20th century. It seems that intense and positive psychological processes can slow down the telomeres' shortening. Mindfulness may also directly increase positive stress arousal states.

There is data linking telomere length to cognitive stress and stress arousal and through research conducted in this area, Dr. Elizabeth Blackburn (UCSF)was awarded a Nobel Prize in Physiology and Medicine in 2009 for her scientific research into meditation and especially mindfulness meditation which she conducted at Buddhist retreats. Her research was conducted together with science colleagues Carol Greider (Johns Hopkins) and Jack Szostak (Harvard). Their research into the biological significance of telomeres and telomerase are a major part of the emerging keys to ageing, life span and health span. Undeniably, meditation has proven to be very effective at slowing telomere loss. [27, 28, 29]

The New Science of Longevity

How to Regrow Telomeres and Increase Telomerase Naturally

Telomerase activators can be found naturally in plants and have shown to have anti-ageing effects. Such natural telomerase activators are also available as nutritional supplements. [30]

Leading telomere expert and anti-ageing specialist Dr. David Woynarowski PHD, expounded the benefits of telomerase lengthening effect on telomeres in his book "The Immortality Edge".

He claims using himself as a guinea pig as proof in point that it can reset your biologic time clocks and that you can slow down the loss of the telomere segments. This, he says, would slow down ageing, add length to telomere segment and would reverse the ageing process. [31]

Dr. Dave also says: "I have documented dramatic changes in telomere length in the white blood cell compartment, the place we measure telomere lengths. I have documented the increased cellularity and decreased fat content in my own bone marrow and that of several of my stem cell patients.

Your List Of Wholefoods To Reverse Ageing

Recommended Telomere Support Superherbs	Antioxidants and Telomere Support Superfoods
Ashwagandha root extract (withania somnifera)	Acacia bark extract (acacia nilotica)
Asian ginseng root extract (panax ginseng)	Black tea leaf extract (camellia sinensis)
Bacopa extract (bacopa monnieri)	Chia seed extract (salvia hispanica)
Bilberry fruit extract (vaccinium myrtillus)	Chinese goldthread rhizome extract (copies chinensis)
Blueberry fruit extract (vaccinium angustifolium)	Harada fruit extract (terminalia chebula)
Boswellia fruit extract (boswellia serrata)	Hawthorn fruit extract (crataegus pinnatifida)
Curcumin or Turmeric root extract (curcuma longa)	Hawthorn root extract (crataegus pinnatifida)
Grape seed extract (vitis vinifera)	Maca root extract (lepidium meyenii)
Green tea extract (carnellia sinensis)	Plantain leaf extract (plantago major)
Horny goat weed (epimedium sagittatum)	Quercetin
Milk thistle extract (silybum marianum)	Shilajit extract
Pomegranate fruit extract (punica granatum)	Velvet bean root extract (mucuna pruriens)
Red raspberry fruit extract (rubus idaeus)	White tea extract (camellia sinensis)
Resveratrol (Polygonum cuspidatum)	

SUMMARY OF CHAPTER THREE

Telomeres and Anti-ageing

- Anti-Ageing and Telomeres and the man who would stop time
- What are Telomeres? Much more than a biology recap
- How can we reverse ageing?
- The secrets of longevity
- The main accelerators of ageing: THE BIG 3 – Inflammation – Glycation – Methylation
  - o Inflammation and ageing
  - o The solution to reduce inflammation Naturally
  - o Omega-3s are your 3 amigos
  - o Glycation: the issue and the solution
  - o Methylation" The issue and the solution
- Good news: you can control the deceleration of ageing!
- The most important thing you can do is to change your diet
- The big 4 to slow down Telomere reduction: diet – exercise – sleep – meditation
- The New Science of longevity
  - o How to Regrow Telomeres and Increase Telomerase Naturally
  - o Your list of whole foods to reverse ageing

CHAPTER FOUR

Earthing and Rejuvenation

"The old people came literally to love the soil. They sat on the ground with the feeling of being close to a mothering power. It was good for the skin to touch the Earth, and the old people liked to remove their moccasins and walk with their bare feet on the sacred Earth. The soil was soothing, strengthening, cleansing, and healing".

Ota Kte (Luther Standing Bear)
Lakota Sioux writer, educator, and tribal leader.

CHAPTER FOUR

Earthing and Rejuvenation

Bare feet, soles crunching the sand, toes sifting through wet, gritty sand, cool salt water occasionally lapping over my feet, sun on my skin, the clapping sound of the waves from the ocean to my right, the chirpy sounds of birds and rhythmic hypnotising sound of crickets to my left. Bursts of ocean breeze cooling my skin. Paradise?

My body loves it, my mind inhales it all. I have a smile on my face, shaded under a big straw hat.

My body transformed itself after a year of walking on the beach first thing every morning, since I arrived here on the Sunshine Coast. I was one of the last Covid 19 refugees, timely escaping New South Wales before "hard border closure rules" set by the Australian Government in July 2020.

It has already been 10 years since I first read this interesting data about the power of grounding or earthing!

So much happened and halted my progress, starting with my car accident, forcing a shift in my career direction, prompting my studies for a homeopathic medicine degree and eventually having both hips replaced.

Fast forward to today and the amazing ongoing physical and mental transformation I am experiencing with powerful and yet simple

www.TheAgelessExecutive.com

lifestyle changes like walking barefoot on the beach every day.

There is nothing more empowering than starting the first Zoom meeting for the day feeling totally energized and in full control of the day ahead!

Earthing and Body Regeneration

Throughout the ages, various cultures around the world honoured their connection to the energy of Earth in different ways. You probably have heard Traditional Chinese Medicine referring to it as earth Qi and in Indian Ayurveda as Prana.

Earthing, also known as grounding, is the practice of connecting your body to the Earth's subtle electrical field. It involves connecting the body to the Earth's surface energy by walking barefoot on grass, sand, or soil. This connection helps to balance the body's electrical system when having direct physical contact with the vast supply of electrons on the surface of the Earth [1]

Earthing is a simple yet powerful way to improve your overall health and wellbeing This connection has been found to have a wide range of health benefits, including improved sleep quality, reduced inflammation, pain relief and mental benefit.

Earthing is a natural way to help the body regenerate and discharge stress.

Throughout evolution, humans walked barefoot and slept on the ground and received from the Earth a natural, nurturing and gentle electric energy.

Pain and diseases caused by chronic inflammation are a major health concern for many people. The root cause of this inflammation is the presence of free radicals, which are positively charged molecules that can damage cells and tissues. Scientists have found that free radicals can cause oxidative stress, which leads to inflammation and other health problems.

The beauty of earthing / grounding is that when you make direct contact with the Earth by being barefoot outside, the negatively charged electrons from the Earth are absorbed into your body (positively charged) and thus reduce the free radicals and inflammation.

The human immune system evolved over a long span of time during which we were in virtually constant barefoot contact with the Earth.

However, modern lifestyle has increasingly separated humans from this flow of energy and insulative rubber or plastic-soled shoes have cut us off from receiving the electrical impulses emitted by the earth. We no longer walk barefoot or sit, lie down or sleep on the ground as we did in times past.

This disconnection is depriving us from the many physiological and mental benefits of earthing. In recent decades the incidence of chronic diseases, allergies, auto-immune conditions and insomnia has skyrocketed.

This coincides with the immune system functioning less efficiently as humans increasingly separated themselves from the Earth's energy.

Earthing and Natural Therapy Re-Discovery

In the late 1990s, Clint Ober, retired cable TV executive, started to think about the human body in terms of electrical grounding and rediscovered earthing and its surprisingly positive effects on the human body.

Clint later co-authored a book with Martin Zucker and cardiologist
Dr. Stephen Sinatra
"Earthing: The Most Important Health Discovery Ever?"

***"The more time we spend disconnected from the
Earth, the more we feel disconnected from ourselves."***

Clint Ober

For 25 years, they promoted the scientific exploration of earthing
which Jim McFarlane, Associate Professor, University of New
England, wrote about as well. [2]

The human body is mostly water and minerals, which makes it a
good conductor of electricity.

Jim McFarlane said: "Living in an electrically charged environment
means the natural equilibrium of chemical substances is altered and
they don't function as they would when the body is earthed".

"The surface of our planet drains the built-up positive charge from
our body. So, by connecting with our planet's own electrical system,
we can bring ourselves back to a natural state of balance".

Earthing and Science

Dr. Sinatra, cardiologist with 30 years experience in medicine,
observed that earthing, whilst profoundly simple and practical, can
be an effective and cost-cutting way to combat common illnesses
and pain problems [3, 4]

He noted that earthing improved arrhythmias, blood pressure, blood viscosity and flow, and energy production of heart cells. Whilst more research does need to be conducted, earthing may very well be an essential element in the quest to increase human longevity.

Normalising Cortisol Levels and Live Blood Microscopy

Research on Earthing and Cortisol conducted by M. Ghaly, and D. Teplitz demonstrated that sleeping grounded normalizes cortisol level and improves sleep. [5] [6] [7]

Dr. Sinatra also conducted an informal experiment utilizing darkfield microscopy that produced dramatic changes in blood cell aggregation after only 40 minutes of earthing. He considered earthing as a profoundly simple, practical, effective and cost-cutting way to combat common illnesses and pain problems and make people healthier. In his own field of cardiology, he said it has great promise for improving arrhythmias, blood pressure, blood viscosity and flow, and energy production of heart cells [8]

Further benefits highlighted in earthing research has shown protection and reduction of EMFs (electromagnetic frequencies) on the body. [9]

Research on Earthing and Body Regeneration

For more than 20 years, earthing research and feedback from individuals who have grounded themselves, some while sleeping at night, demonstrate a multitude of benefits.

- Electrophysiological measurements have indicated more efficient cardiovascular, respiratory, and nervous system function

- Earthing observation has demonstrated less inflammation and faster recovery from exercise-induced soreness and sometimes even elimination of pain!

- This earthing energy creates a distinct and uplifting shift in our physiology

- An additional benefit is that it promotes health, vitality and better sleep; harmonizes and stabilizes the body's basic biological rhythms; knocks down (and even knocks out) chronic inflammation

- This disconnect from our natural earth resource has proven to be an important factor behind chronic disease in recent decades, and inflammatory-related conditions

- Martin Zucker has written and co-authored fifteen books. His most famous ones are on "Earthing", "Move Yourself (Wiley), "Reverse Heart Disease Now" (Wiley) and "Natural Hormone Balance for Women" (Atria/Pocket Books), all which are proponents of the health benefits of earthing [10]

- Earthing research suggests that free electrons from the earth neutralize the positively charged free radicals that are the hallmark of chronic inflammation. "Can electrons act as antioxidants?" [11]

Spectacular results on lowering BP from earthing

Dr. David Richards, NSW integrative doctor, achieved spectacular results after introducing some of his patients to earthing and commented that he observed that "most people with high blood pressure, thyroid disease and diabetes start to improve [as a result of earthing] and have to reduce their medication," and he added: "Just about every problem I see on a daily basis has some inflammatory component and the beneficial results are generally a result of the anti-inflammatory effects of earthing."

Further research conducted during the last 15 years has demonstrated that grounding (earthing) the human body to Earth's surface charge generates multiple beneficial physiological effects including lowering of high blood pressure (BP). [12]

We are bioelectrical beings living on an electrical planet

We human beings are a collection of dynamic electrical circuits. In the living matrix of our body, trillions of cells constantly transmit and receive energy during their biochemical reactions. So, our heart, brain, nervous system, muscles and immune system are electrical subsystems operating within our "bioelectrical" body.

The movement of nutrients and water into the cells is regulated by electric fields.

Body Electric

Dr. Robert O. Becker was a pioneer in the field of bioelectric science and presented a fascinating look at the role electricity plays in healing the body and how it fights disease and harnesses the body's healing powers. His book "The Body Electric" presents his research including that all our movements, behaviours, and actions are energized by electricity. [13]

His initial discovery seems to support the theory of an immediate electrophysiological shift inside our body when earthing, or connection to the Earth. Indeed, earthing research shows improved blood, improved nervous system, improved immune system, and improved muscular function.

Earthing and the Eradication of Inflammation

The body is a good conductor of free electrons.

When people are grounded through the feet, either by standing barefoot on the Earth or via grounded EKG patches in experiments, they sometimes feel a tingling sensation moving up the legs. (EKG or ECG patches are electrocardiogram electrodes that stick to the skin and are placed on certain body locations and attached to an ECG machine to measure or monitor heart health). This tingling phenomenon is known as the "grounding effect" and it occurs when electrons move up into your body. It is believed that this effect can have a positive impact on our health and wellbeing as it helps to balance out the electrical charge in our body.

The speed of this activity was "clocked" as taking about 20 to 30 minutes to reach sites of pain and inflammation and then begin neutralizing the inflammation.

Free radicals are molecules that can cause damage to cells and tissues in the body, leading to inflammation and pain.

Electrons are essential components of our bodies and play a vital role in many biological processes. They are attracted to sites with a positive charge, such as free radicals, which are involved in the inflammatory process. This attraction helps to neutralize the free radicals and reduce inflammation. As a result, electrons can help to reduce pain and improve overall health.

In clinical studies, the physiological effects of earthing have been almost immediate.

The body settles and equalizes electrically to the ground potential almost instantaneously.

The information that a new potential has been established in the body is transmitted, also almost instantaneously, to the autonomic nervous system which then responds by "adjusting" electrical activities throughout the body.

Muscle tension, skin conductance and brain waves, are adjusted in a few seconds at the most!

Earthing as an Anti-Ageing Strategy

It is now becoming apparent that the immune system undergoes age-associated alterations or immune-senescence. [14]

One of the causes of general deterioration during ageing is free radical damage, oxidative stress, causing injury to cells.

Since earthing greatly reduces oxidative stress and inflammation, it is expected to increase life expectancy and improve health.

Maintaining a functionally "young" immune system is an excellent strategy for preserving the quality of life and slowing senescence.

Thousands of people around the world—men, women, children and particularly athletes—have incorporated earthing into their daily routines and report that they sleep better, have less pain and stress, and experience faster recovery from trauma.

Earthing your body synchronizes your internal biological clocks, hormonal cycles and physiological rhythms.

Earthing suffuses your body with the healing of negatively charged free electrons on the surface of the Earth.

The Benefits of Earthing

For more than twenty years, earthing research and feedback from individuals who have grounded themselves, primarily while sleeping at night, demonstrate a multitude of benefits.

Together with my research and an excellent website called "Better Earthing", here is a list of incredible benefits from such a simple natural practice. [15]

- Improvement or elimination of the symptoms of many inflammation-related disorders which cause ageing
- Reduction or elimination of chronic pain
- Better sleep and faster to get to sleep
- Increased energy
- Lowered stress, more calmness by cooling down the nervous system and stress hormones, a great way to rejuvenate your body
- Normalisation of the body's biological rhythms
- Thinner blood, improved blood pressure and flow
- Relief for muscle tension and headache
- Lessened hormonal and menstrual symptoms
- Reduction/elimination of jet lag
- Protection against environmental electromagnetic fields (EMFs)
- Accelerated recovery from intense athletic activity

How to start Earthing

Find the nearest patch of earth and kick your shoes off.
Wet or damp sand and grass provide optimum earthing.
Go barefoot as much as possible, whenever possible

If this is not possible, there are other alternatives with earthing products:

- Mattress covers
- Mats to put under your desk
- Wristbands
- Earthing blankets
- Specially designed footwear

Earthing is the most natural thing in the world.

SUMMARY OF CHAPTER FOUR
Earthing & Regeneration

- Earthing and Body Regeneration
- What do rubber soles have to do with inflammation?
- Earthing and natural therapy Re-discovery
- Earthing and science
- Normalizing cortisol levels and live blood microscopy
- Research on Earthing and Body Regeneration
- Spectacular results on lowering BP from earthing
- We are bioelectrical beings living on an electrical planet
- The body electric
- Earthing and the eradication of inflammation
- Earthing as anti-ageing strategy
- Earthing and your biological clock
- The benefits of Earthing
- How to start Earthing

CHAPTER FIVE

The Miracle of Brain Rejuvenation

"*When your brain works right, you are right.*

When your brain has trouble, you have trouble in your life.

The health of your brain affects your life."

Dr Daniel Amen

CHAPTER FIVE

The Miracle of Brain Rejuvenation

Your brain is the most sophisticated organ in the universe. It is one of the most complex and fascinating structures in the world, composed of over 100 billion nerve cells, or neurons, and each neuron can form thousands of connections with other neurons. This incredible network of neurons allows us to think, feel, remember, learn and experience the world around us. Through neuroscience research we are beginning to understand how our brains work and how we can use this knowledge to improve our lives.

> **There are more connections in your brain than there are stars in the Universe!**

With scientific knowledge and a few simple tweaks you can greatly improve your brain health and leadership effectiveness. Indeed, the power of a healthy brain in leadership and its impact on the workforce can be extraordinary!

SPECT Imaging and the Brain

One of the world's most passionate advocate for brain health is Dr. Daniel Amen who with a SPECT imaging database containing more than 160,000 brain scans, is the leader in applying imaging in everyday clinical psychiatric practice. [1]

SPECT is brain imaging study that looks at blood flow and activity patterns. It shows 3 things: areas of the brain that work well, areas of the brain that are low in activity and areas of the brain that are too high in activity.

Dr. Amen is a double board-certified psychiatrist, clinical neuroscientist, brain imaging specialist, distinguished fellow of the American Psychiatric Association and New York Times bestselling author. Dr. Amen is a child and adult psychiatrist and brain scanning imaging specialist who, with his scientists in his clinic, has conducted more than 87,000 brain scans. He lives and breathes "optimising brain health".

He is probably the strongest influencer in the world in this area of brain health and the content of his books and 70 published scientific papers presents research that is crucial for brain rejuvenation and optimal brain functioning.

At one of his conferences he presented his audience with a study and rehabilitation program he worked with of active and retired NFL Players who underwent SPECT imaging displaying damage seen across the whole brain.

He reminds us that the skull is hard for a good reason, which is to protect the brain because the brain is as soft as butter, so even though there is solid protection for the brain, it still can be impacted by a fall, an accident or impact sport like football or boxing. So, can football cause long term brain damage? Hell yes!!

So, when Dr. Amen put those players through a brain smart program, 87% of them improved in areas of blood flow, memory and mood, proving that you are not stuck with the brain you have. You can make it better on the right program.

How exciting is that??? Reversing brain damage is a new frontier with much wider implications.

I would strongly suggest that you read at least one of Dr. Daniel Amen's books!

Some of my favourites are.

- *Change Your Brain, Change your life*
- *Use Your Brain to Change your life*
- *You can Improve your Brain*
- *Healing Anxiety and Depression*
- *Healing ADD*
- *Making a Good Brain Great*
- *The Brain in Love*

Brain Scans Measure Health

Brain scans are becoming increasingly important in the medical field as they can provide valuable insights into a person's health. This technology can be also used to measure mental health such as depression and anxiety, but most importantly as a mean to monitor one's progress when engaged in improving one's health.

They can also help us understand how our brains work and how we can optimise them for better performance. By understanding the physical health of the organ between our ears, we can make sure that we are living life to its fullest potential.

Brain and Food

The human brain represents 2% of your body weight, on average about 3 pounds (1.3Kgs).

> **It is only when it comes to the brain that size matters!**
>
> *Edua Potor*

When the body is at rest — not engaged in any activity besides the basics of breathing, digesting and keeping itself warm — we know that the brain uses up a startling 20% to 25% of the body's overall energy, mainly in the form of **glucose**. That translates to 350 or 450 calories per day for the average woman or man, respectively. [2]

Your brain is always "on". It takes care of your thoughts and movements, of your breathing and heartbeat, your senses — it works hard 24/7, even while you're asleep. This means it requires a constant supply of fuel which comes from the foods you eat, So, what you eat directly affects the structure and function of your brain and, ultimately, your mood. [3]

> **How you think is directly related to how you eat**
>
> *Edua Potor*

Brain Nutrition Simplified

We have covered hydration in the first chapter and nutrition in the second chapter as they are the foundations of a healthy brain. We can further tweak this to enhance and optimise brain health.

Maintain good hydration because the brain is 80% water and even the slightest level of dehydration will raise stress hormones which are damaging to the brain.

Decrease your caloric intake, as highlighted by substantial research, resulting in an increase in nerve growth factors. Make sure you make the quality of every calorie count! [4]

A diet rich in omega-3s is crucial to the brain. Eating fish (preferably wild caught salmon) and taking fish oil will help promoting DHA, which is so good for retina health, mood balancing and supporting the health of the brain synapses. [4]

Increase your intake of antioxidants with a diet of wholefoods from fruit and vegetables to mitigate cognitive decline. The US Department of Agriculture suggests: all Berries, Broccoli, Beets, Avocados, Oranges, Red Grapes, Capsicum, Cherries and Kiwis.

Having proteins at each meal will help balance blood sugar levels and a simple thing such as adding nuts will help to prevent brain fog which is associated with eating simple carbohydrates, such as baked treats, fruit juice concentrate and breakfast cereal. [5]

Is Sugar a Food?

Sugar Blues and the Decline of Civilizations

Our overall physical health and mental health is greatly affected by ingesting refined sugar and yet it is the most widely consumed dietary ingredient. In his book "Sugar Blues", William Dufty writes about the history of sugar in connection with the decline of civilizations when a society incorporates sugar in their diet. He also vehemently criticizes the sugar industry for misrepresenting the health and safety data of its products. [6]

Over 1.6 million copies of his book have been printed, which highlights the fact that there are many people who have become more conscious of the way in which unnatural foods are affecting our health and our brain! In his book, originally printed in the 1970s, Dufty plays the role of whistle blower presenting alarming statistics about the rate at which every American consumes sugar every year and at that time it was one hundred pounds (45.36Kgs) per person per year! He further states that sugar is as addictive as nicotine.

And of more recent times, sugar has been compared to cocaine addiction as published by a large American insurance company. (Term Life Insurance).

Speed of Thinking

Have you ever wondered how quickly information travels in your brain? It turns out that on average, information in your brain travels at an incredible speed of 268 miles per hour unless you are drunk or smoking pot.

It is a well-known fact that we lose around 85,000 neurons every day. This can be a cause of concern for many people as it can lead to cognitive decline and other neurological issues. However, the good news is that our behaviour has the power to either accelerate or decelerate this process. By making healthy lifestyle choices and engaging in activities that stimulate our brains, we can slow down the rate at which we lose neurons and maintain our cognitive health.

Brain health is essential for innovation and creativity. A healthy brain can help us think more clearly, come up with new ideas and solve problems more quickly. It can also help us stay focused on our goals and make better decisions. As such, it is important to take care of our brains to maximize our potential for innovation. This means getting enough sleep, eating a balanced diet, exercising regularly and engaging in activities that stimulate the mind. By taking care of our brains, we can ensure that we are able to think more clearly and make better decisions with the challenges we face in life and in business.

Causes for Alzheimer's

A concerning number of 401,300 people were diagnosed with Alzheimer's in 2022, in Australia and this number is projected to reach more than half a million by 2030. Alzheimer's is a disease which has become a global health crisis and the 6th leading cause of death.

An estimated 6.5 million Americans are living with Alzheimer's disease This is one of the biggest global health crises of the 21st Century

Research indicates that exposure to air pollutants, certain chemicals found in water and food, and even some lifestyle factors can all cause the development of Alzheimer's disease and contribute to the rapid rise of this illness.

Alzheimer's disease starts 30 to 40 years before showing the symptoms, so look after your brain NOW!

As the population continues to live longer, there is an increased risk of developing Alzheimer's disease. This is because the longer a person lives, the more time they have for Alzheimer's to manifest itself. It is important to be aware of the signs and symptoms of this disease, so that it can be diagnosed and treated as soon as possible. Early diagnosis and treatment can help slow down its progression and improve the quality of life for those affected by it. [7]

Weight and the Brain - When Size Matters

Normal weight or overweight brain?

It is well established that obesity has a negative impact on physical health, but recent research has also shown that it can have a detrimental effect on cognitive function as well. Over 140 studies have demonstrated that as your weight goes up, the size and function of your brain goes down. This means that obesity can lead to decreased memory, slower reaction times and difficulty with problem solving. Additionally, it can increase the risk of developing dementia and other neurological disorders. [8] [9] [10]

So, in summary, as your weight goes up, the size and function of your brain goes down!

In overweight people with a BMI over 30, 8% will have less brain tissue and their brain will look 16 years older than healthy people [11]

Results from a cardiovascular health study have shown that obesity is also associated with a lower resting oxygen saturation. [12] Obviously less oxygen in the body is less oxygen to arteries, to the heart and to the brain!

Your Brain Runs Your Life

The brain receives information from the outside world through our five senses and connects the messages in a way that has meaning for us, controls innumerable functions such as thoughts, memory, speech, movement of our limbs and our organs, and of course our basic life functions such as excretion, metabolism, reproduction etc.

Success always starts with a good healthy brain.

Edua Potor

Your brain functionality		
Parietal Lobe	Visual functions	Reading Understanding Language
Occipital Lobe	Vision	Light, colours, images
Cerebellum	Motor	Balance - coordination - movement
Brain Stem	Basic life functions	Excretion – metabolism - reproduction
Temporal Lobe	Memories	Tactile - sound
Frontal Lobe	Thinking	Problem solving, creative thinking, personality

Your Behaviour Could Damage Your Brain

Your behaviour could be causing damage to your brain and it could be causing acceleration of the ageing process. Of course, the flip side of the coin is that your behaviour could also decelerate the speed of your ageing which is the most exciting part of what you have control over.

Unfortunately, food manufacturers and society keep trying to shove bad food down your throat.

This is why you need to create strong reasons to become and stay healthy.

Care about the health of your brain!

The Brain Can Rejuvenate Itself

Brain scans have proven that the brain can rejuvenate itself.

The future of healthcare is shifting towards natural treatments and therapies, as opposed to the easy use of pharmaceuticals. This trend is driven by the increasing awareness of the potential side effects of pharmaceuticals, as well as the growing popularity of alternative treatments such as acupuncture, herbal remedies and homeopathy.

In less fortunate countries, people often have limited access to healthcare and medical treatments. This means that they must rely on natural methods to regain and maintain their health. These methods are often cheaper than traditional treatments but require more effort and dedication from the individual. Our reliance on quick fixes and medication has produced weaker beings and secondary side effects affecting the brain.

Next time you have a headache, rather than reaching for an aspirin, you may find that drinking a glass of water will alleviate the pressure. Your brain will thank you for it!

Oxygen, Your Brain, and Ageing (or not)

Do you want significant increase in the quality of your life?

Anything that decreases the flow of blood and oxygen to your brain, ages you.

Edua Potor

Did you know that there are 100,000 miles of blood vessels in the brain? It makes it so much more obvious as to why keeping optimum blood flow and oxygen levels are crucial to a well-functioning brain!

Generally, poor blood flow and low oxygen levels to your brain will cause premature ageing and are often caused by lifestyle choices such as smoking, drinking alcohol, poor diet and not getting enough sleep. This includes being sedentary and exercising less than twice a week. [13]

> **Change your brain, change your age.**
>
> *Edua Potor*

How to Increase Oxygen to your Brain

Even if you breathe "normally", your brain may not be getting enough oxygen and in fact, the brain uses three times as much oxygen as muscles in the body do! [14]

Brain cells don't survive longer than 4 to 5 minutes without oxygen!

How can we ensure that we do not subject our brain to slow oxygen starvation over the years?

1- Yoga

Studies have shown that yoga enhances pulmonary functions, especially the cobra pose which stretches your abdomen and strengthens around your shoulders, arms, and back muscles and opens your chest. It is easy to perform and provides myriad benefits.

Here is an easy description of this pose, curtesy of Yoga Journal: [15]

- Begin on your belly with your feet hip-distance apart and your hands beside your ribs

- Extend your big toes straight back and press down with all ten toenails to activate your quadriceps

- Rotate your inner thighs toward the ceiling to broaden the lower back

- Pressing down lightly with your hands, start to lift your head and chest, rolling your shoulders back and down

- Keep the back of your neck long and focus on lifting your sternum instead of lifting your chin

- Straighten your arms while keeping your shoulders remaining away from your ears. Keep at least a slight bend in your elbows

- To exit the pose, release back to your mat

2- **Take short Walks** throughout the day.
5 to 10 minutes will increase blood circulation and positively impact on the brain.

3- **Breathe through your nose,** engage the diaphragm in your abdomen which will result in bringing more oxygen to your blood.

4- **Stand UP!** A study published by the Oxford University Press journal "Brain" reports that standing up activates cerebral circulation. [16] [17]

Scientists and the Brain

Dr. Michael Colgan PH.D., a research scientist and leading sport nutritionist, runs The Colgan Institute of Nutritional Science. [18] He is one of the world's scientific experts on the inhibition of ageing with the effects of nutrition and exercise on athletic performance, prevention of chronic degenerative disease and prevention of degeneration of the brain and has written more than 50 scientific papers on nutrition. [19]

More importantly, he affirms that the quality of the protein you eat determines the quality of the proteins that compose all the muscles that move you and all the brain cells that operate your mind [20]

Develop Brain envy ☺

Dr. Daniel Amen

Advice from Dr. Colgan

- High quality vitamin, high fish oil and brain enhancement supplements
- Vit D – to support heart health and help preventing depression, Alzheimer's and overweight
- Physical exercise at the rate of 45 min 4x week
- Lift weight 2x week
- Physical health = emotional health
- Building muscles to build testosterone because lack of testosterone is associated with memory problems, depression and ageing

Summary and Important Tips for the Health of Your Brain

Don't put yourself at risk of injury. Remember that the skull is hard but brain is soft. Contact sports might not be brain friendly.

Make rational health choices with drugs and alcohol.

Be aware of your weight fluctuations (upwards); your weight affects your brain.

Address issues you may suffer from that cause insomnia – or sleep apnoea.

Keep the amount of caffeine and nicotine in check.

This will be challenging to some: if you don't use your phone, turn it off!

Get rid of sugar in your diet! Gentlemen, be aware that sugar lowers testosterone!

As always, food can be poison or food can be medicine.

Remember that your brain is involved in everything you do: How you think – feel – act – interact – plan – judge – make decisions.

Chronic stress: Who do you spend time with?

The health of the people you spend time with will impact on your longevity.

Be part of a supportive community.

Exercise your brain, stretch your brain: you want to learn new and different things.

Avoid brain fatigue, make one decision at a time - not thirty as it can impair your judgement.

Breathe deeper.

Practise meditation.

Thoughts are real - your brain can expand and has unlimited capacities to grow.

You can accelerate or decelerate the ageing process of your brain with what you eat!

Stop eating toxic food: eat only quality foods.

Remember that medical students are still getting less than 20 hours education about nutrition over 4 years. Don't solely depend on medical advice.

It is predicted that brain scans will become as common as colonoscopy.

The neurofeedback system can generate amazing images from EEGs (Electroencephalography). Be the one who is proud to watch pictures of your beautiful brain.

SUMMARY OF CHAPTER FIVE
The Miracle of Brain Rejuvenation

- The most sophisticated organ in the Universe
- The leading brain expert in the USA – SPECT Imaging and the Brain
- Brain Scans measure Health
- Brain and Food
- Is Sugar a food? – Sugar Blues and the decline of civilizations
- The speed of thinking
- Causes for Alzheimer's
- Weight and your brain – When size matters
- Your brain runs your life
- Your behavior could damage your brain
- The brain can rejuvenate itself
- Oxygen, your brain, and ageing (or not)
- How to increase Oxygen to your brain
- Scientists and the Brain
- Advice from Dr. Colgan
- Summary and Important tips for the health of your brain

CHAPTER SIX

The Brain and Epigenetics – Mitochondria – Psychiatry

"If it is good for your brain, it is good for every part and function of your body."

Edua Potor

CHAPTER SIX

The Brain and Epigenetics – Mitochondria – Psychiatry

Genus versus environment – The Science of Epigenetics

Epigenetics is a rapidly growing field of science which studies how environmental factors can influence gene expression. It has been found that genes can increase your risk of receptivity to an ailment. However, even if you have the genetic predisposition for a particular ailment, your lifestyle choices and environment can still play a role in whether you develop it. Several factors in the environment speak to your DNA and will turn genes on or off. When genes are turned on they are more active and when they are off they are silent. Your gene sequence can change your phenotype, which is the appearance and performance of the body. Healthy phenotype is called 'wild type': healthy, robust and disease resistant. BUT the environment can change this state of health into inflammation, sickness and disease. It also puts a mark on your DNA without changing its sequence. [1] [2] [3]

Our environment, including what we eat, the supplements we take, the exercise we do, the meditation we practice and our lifestyle choices all have an impact on our epigenetic expression.

Siobhán Dunphy, a PhD in regenerative medicine, explains in the European Scientist "Changes in DNA sequences can take millions of years to appear, whereas epigenetic changes happen much faster and can occur within one generation." [4]

Recent studies have shown that our genes "listen" to the environment in ways that can have a direct impact on our health and behaviour. Our diets, lifestyle choices and even the air we breathe can influence how our genes express themselves. [5]

Research has shown that your environment can be up to 80% responsible for what happens to you and your health.

This is probably one of the most exciting scientific discoveries of all; you are in control of 80% of your future!

You can change the expression of your genes by changing your lifestyle, changing your diet, altering what you ingest.

In the animal kingdom there is a great example of this phenomenon in bees. The bees that are fed with royal jelly become queen bees - they all have the same genetic makeup, the same genome, but the ingestion of "supplements" make them become queen bees! [6] [7]

The queen bee only eats royal jelly resulting in extraordinary longevity as she can live approximately forty times longer than a worker bee!

Moreover, royal jelly increases blood flow by more than 100 times compared to honey, so it improves metabolism and may improve biological resistance and immunity. [7]

This striking illustration of epigenetics effects was not lost on ancient Greeks who were the first to describe royal jelly as part of the nectar of the gods.

You Can Control Your Cells' Environment

What are those environmental factors and which ones can you control?

Eating a balanced diet is essential for our bodies to function properly. Food provides us with the vitamins, minerals, essential fats and antioxidants that our cells need to stay healthy and alive. These nutrients, eaten from a variety of foods from all groups, are necessary for our bodies to remain healthy and to maintain energy levels throughout the day.

Conversely, if the quality or type of food eaten is not wholesome or not optimised, our body will not be provided with the required building blocks and the chemistry provided will not be supportive to health. Molecules will not be offered what they need and this leads to the foundation of chronic disease.

There are several major factors that can have a negative impact on our brain health, which is essential for our overall wellbeing, yet many of us are unaware of the major obstacles that can prevent us from achieving it. The most important and specific culprits eroding our brain health are sugar, gluten, toxins and lack of physical activity.

Major Obstacle 1 – Sugar

- In 1700, we ate less than 5 kg of sugar/year
- In 2000, we ate 70 kg of sugar a year
- All this sugar is interfering with providing the building blocks of a healthy life
- Sugar also speaks to your DNA, turning genes on or off, shifting a healthy phenotype into a sickly one

- Sugar increases the risk for high blood pressure, obesity, diabetes, heart disease, neurological problems, autoimmunity and cancer

- Australians have become the highest sugar consumers in the world!

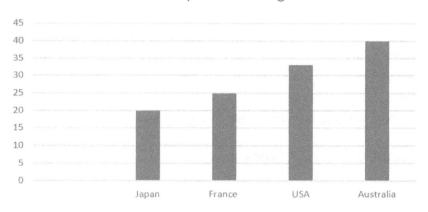

Average consumption of sugar per year, per person in Kilograms

Published by "Food and Agriculture Organization of the United States" in 2015

US Sugar Consumption, 1822 - 2005

Published in "Australian Business Insider" in 2013

Major Obstacle 2 - Gluten

For those who are genetically vulnerable, food can be a source of serious health problems. One such problem is the abnormal elevation of immune cells and increased inflammation caused by gluten. Gluten is a protein found in wheat, barley and rye that can cause an autoimmune reaction in some people. This reaction can lead to digestive issues, fatigue, joint pain and brain fog. [8]

Gluten has been linked to neurological problems, mental health issues and autoimmunity disorders. In some cases it can even switch the wild phenotype into a sickly one. [9] This means that people who are genetically predisposed to certain diseases may be more likely to develop them if they consume gluten-rich foods.

Major Obstacle 3 - Toxins

Since the end of World War Two, the world has seen an unprecedented increase in the number of chemicals registered for use. In total, over 80,000 different chemicals have been registered and are now used in a variety of industries and applications. This has had a profound effect on our environment and our health, as many of these chemicals have been found to be hazardous to both humans and animals.

Recent studies have revealed that 200 synthetic compounds are present in the umbilical cord blood of newborns and in the breast milk of their mothers! These compounds, which are not naturally occurring, can be found in everyday products such as plastics, cosmetics and food packaging.

Epigenetics – Reprogram Your Future!

The premise of epigenetics states that our diet can influence how our genes are expressed. Eating a balanced wholesome diet full of nutrient-rich foods is essential to maintain optimal health and prevent disease. It is critical for providing us with the energy we need to live life to its fullest, allowing us to be more productive and creative for longer.

Dr. Dave Woynarowski, one of the world's top anti-ageing specialist, is author of a book on telomeres called "The Immortality Edge". [10] [11] His book is based on Nobel Prize–winning genetic research; a simple plan to keep your telomeres healthy for better health and longevity.

Together with his understanding of the principles of epigenetics, Dr. Dave recommends the following:

- Reduce omega-6 intake to reduce inflammation
- Increase omega-3 (Fish Oil) to help your body heal itself and reduce inflammation
- Moderately intense exercise 30 mins five times/week
- Meditate 20 mins/day; this will rebalance Para/sympathetic outflow
- Sleep quality: at least 7 hours to rebalance your hormones naturally
- Eat an organic plant-based diet with inclusion of grass-fed meat, free range chicken, wild fish
- Look after your skin, the largest organ of your body

It is worth pointing out that just as Dr. Dave puts anti-inflammation on top of his list, so do many health specialists. Even though inflammation is a natural response of the body to protect itself from injury or infection, it is when it becomes chronic that it presents a real problem, leading to a variety of health issues and age-related illnesses.

The three most serious health threats associated with inflammation are Heart Disease, Cancer and Dementia.

Dr. Barry Sears' book "The Anti-inflammation Zone" denounces the dangers of the silent epidemic that is destroying our health. [12]

One of the easiest ways to reverse inflammation within 30 days is to adhere to an anti-inflammation diet.

If you want to think better, perform better, look better and feel better, then it's important to make sure that you are eating the right foods. This list of anti-Inflammation foods will help you to do just that!

90 Anti inflammation foods A-Z chart					
Alfalfa	Bok choy	Cherries	Green Cabbage	Onion	Shiitake mushrooms
Alfalfa grass	Broccoli	Chives	Green Tea	Oranges	Seaweed
Almonds	Brussel Sprouts	Cilantro	Horseradish root	Oregano	Sesame seeds
Almond butter	Buckwheat	Coconut – fresh	Jicama	Papaya	Spelt
Apple cider vinegar	Cabbage	Cucumber	Kale	Parsnips	Spinach
Artichoke	Cantaloupe	Cumin seeds	Kamut	Peas – fresh	Sprouted seeds
Asparagus	Caraway seeds	Egg plant	Kelp	Pineapple	Squash

Avocado	Carrots	Endives	Leeks	Pumpkin	Sweet potatoes
Barley grass	Cauliflower	Fennel	Lemon - fresh	Quinoa	Tomatoes
Basil	Cayenne Pepper	Fennel seeds	Lentils	Red beets – fresh	Turmeric
Bee pollen	Cinnamon	Flaxseed	Lettuce	Red Cabbage	Turnip
Bell peppers	Curry Powder	Figs	Limes – fresh	Red radish	Wheatgrass
Black Beans	Broccoli	Garlic -fresh	Mustard greens	Salmon- wild	White radish
Black radish	Brussel Sprouts	Ginger - fresh	Navy beans	Savoy cabbage	Yam
Blueberries	Cherries	Grapefruit pink & red	Oats	Sea Vegies	Zucchini

The Brain and Mitochondria

The Importance of Well-Functioning Mitochondria for a Healthy Brain

Mitochondria are the most important organelles inside the cells and the prime source and manager of energy supply for each cell. By promoting optimum mitochondrial health, we are supporting superior functioning of every cell and system in our body and keep our brain healthy and sharp.

When it is not working well, it can lead to several neurological diseases such as Huntington's disease, Parkinson's disease and Alzheimer's disease but this mitochondrial shrinking can be halted with Fish Oil, Creatine and Co-enzyme Q10. [13]

How does it work?

Myelin is an essential component of the nervous system, acting as an insulation sheet around the axon of a neuron. It plays a vital role in proper functioning of the nervous system by allowing electrical signals to travel quickly and efficiently between neurons. Myelin also helps to increase the speed at which signals travel along axons, allowing for faster communication between neurons, helps protect neurons from damage and helps them regenerate after injury. As such, it is essential for proper functioning of the nervous system and for maintaining healthy brain function.

A synapse, also known as a neuronal junction, serves as the point where electric nerve impulses are transmitted between two nerve cells (neurons) or from one neuron to another. Rather than being characterized as a process, a synapse represents a critical location for the transmission of these impulses. This synaptic connection forms the foundation for inter-neuronal communication, enabling essential functions such as cognition, movement, emotions, as well as the processes of learning and memory formation.

Neurotransmitters are chemicals that transmit signals across a synapse from one neuron (brain cell) to another 'target' neuron. To ensure that the brain can produce enough neurotransmitters, it needs certain nutrients such as sulphur, B6 and antioxidants.

Recent research in brain cell biology is providing substantial evidence that mitochondria, the powerhouses of the cell, are a major source (90-95%) of free radicals within the cell. Mitochondria help turn the energy we take from food into energy that the cell can use. It appears that several agents have shown to be beneficial

in protecting neurons, such as Vits B1 (thymine), B9 (Folate) B12 (Cobalt), omega-3 Fatty Acids, Iodine, Coenzyme Q10. [14]

It is important to maintain a high level of nutrition and a balanced lifestyle to provide the necessary nutrients for optimal mitochondrial functioning. Additionally, caloric restriction has been shown to be an effective way to improve mitochondrial health and function. [15]

A Story of Brain Redemption

Dr. Terry Wahls is a professor of medicine at the University of Iowa who, through her own personal experience with MS, has developed a diet and lifestyle program that has helped her beat the disease. [16] Her story is an inspiring example of how we can take control of our health and make positive changes in our lives. With brain nutrition she was able to move out of her wheelchair to get walking again and even took up cycling. With her new diet and lifestyle change, she resolved her fatigue, eliminated pain, improved her mood, normalised her blood pressure and her blood sugar, lost weight and her declining need for medication soon became zero. She was able to achieve all this within the span of one year!

Dr. Wahls' philosophy is very much based on looking for the root of the problems and not just the symptoms and how a nutrient rich diet can reverse MS and other ailments.

Her research looked at the causes of other brain diseases such as Alzheimer's, Parkinson's, ALS and Huntington's.

Here is the important connection of her discovery with the significance of the function of the mitochondria which stop working in each disease, leading to brain cell death and brain shrinkage! [17]

> **"A healthy brain is the foundation of a well-lived life."**
> Unknown

Food Plan for Mitochondria and your Brain Nutrition

Dr. Wahls' protocol suggests foods fall within 3 groups that are necessary to stimulate enzymes for the processing and elimination of toxins.

I have added some research-based data related to mitochondria health support.

1- Vegetable kingdom - Daily
The plant kingdom is by far the largest one to consider first.

- 3 cups of green leaves:
  Kale is one of the greens that has the most nutrition per calorie than any other plant.

  It also lowers the risk of cataracts and macular degeneration, is a natural toxin removal and a powerful brain booster. [18]

- 3 cups of bright coloured antioxidants from:
  Vegetables: carrots, beets, peppers

  Fruits: berries, peaches, oranges

- 3 cups of sulphur-rich vegetables:
  Cabbage family is rich in sulphur – cabbage, broccoli, cauliflower, kale, radishes.

  Onion family, rich in sulphur: onion, garlic, leeks, chives, shallots.

Mushrooms are also rich in sulphur and so are asparagus.

The brain and the mitochondria need sulphur.

Your liver and kidneys need sulphur to remove toxins from your blood stream.

2- Animal Kingdom - Weekly

Eating organic grass-fed meat is recommended for its health benefits. Organic meat is free from antibiotics and hormones and is produced in a way that respects animal welfare. Grass-fed animals are also healthier than those fed on grain. Eating organic grass-fed meat can help you to maintain a healthy lifestyle while also supporting sustainable farming practices. Organ meats like liver are suggested to be incredibly nutritious and healthy. (19)

3- Ocean Kingdom - Weekly

Wild Fish for omega-3 fatty acids and seaweed are two of the most important sources of iodine and selenium in our diets. Iodine is essential for proper thyroid function, and it can also help to remove toxins and eliminate lead and mercury (heavy metals) from our bodies. Iodine lowers risk of breast cancer and prostate cancer.

Supplements for Mitochondria Health

Dr. Wahls' recommendations:

- Vitamin A: for immune system
- Vitamins B6 and B12: will protect your brain and mitochondria
- Vitamin C: protects your immune cells
- Vitamin K: keeps blood vessels and bones healthy

- C.K: blood vessels and bones healthy minerals
- Minerals are co-factors for 100s of different enzymes in your body.

Diets recommended by health organizations and professionals can be confusing and an analysis of 70 diet plans created to improve nutrient intake suggests that you would need to consume more than 18,000 calories per day to ensure an adequate intake of all essential micronutrients! [20]

Using a high-quality comprehensive vitamin and mineral formula is a powerful way to cover your nutritional bases and correct common nutritional deficiencies that frequently contribute to mitochondrial dysfunction, fatigue and poor health. [21]

So, out of a very long list of supplements for mitochondrial health, [21] here are a few handpicked for you to consider:

- AcetylL-carnitine (ALCAR) - the "mitochondrial rejuvenator"
- Riboflavin
- Creatine: cellular growth and repair
- Taurine: protein synthesis
- N-Acetyl-Cysteine (NAC): increasing glutathione concentrations and preserves cellular health
- D-Ribose: cellular energy production
- Panax Ginseng: protect mitochondria from oxidative damage and improve energy production
- Co-enzyme Q10: essential antioxidant
- Green Tea

- Quercetin: bioflavonoid found in many fruits and vegetables, particularly onions and apples. Potent antioxidant and anti-inflammatory

- Resveratrol: phytochemical found primarily in grape skins and wine

- Pomegranates: reduce blood lipid oxidation and the accumulation of plaque in arteries

- Spirulina: powerful superfood for heart, liver, intestines, and mitochondrial health

- Chlorella: carotenoids, antioxidants, and enzymes to create energy, minimize oxidative stress and neutralize toxicants

- Niacin: Increases NAD

- Glucosamine: powerful longevity supplement

- Calcium AKG: necessary for the electron transport chain to produce cellular energy. (Reduce your biological age by 8 years!)

Foods to Avoid

Be aware of grains, potatoes, and dairy. They create a wide variety of health problems: eczema, asthma, infertility, irritable bowel, fibromyalgia, chronic fatigue, arthritis, chronic headache, neurological complications and behavioural issues.

20 Superfoods for Your Brain and Mitochondria

Nuts/Fruits/Spices/Herbs	Vegetables/Oils/Animal produce Sulphur/drink
Almonds	Kale
Cashew Nuts	Sweet Potato
Walnuts	Coconut Oil
Dark Chocolate	Olive Oil
Coffee	Turkey
Avocado	Eggs
Apple	Salmon
Blueberries	Shirataki Noodle (Yam) (miracle noodle)
Cinnamon	Onion or cabbage or broccoli
Oregano	Green Tea

The Brain and Psychiatry:
Lack of Nutrients Causing Brain Damage

Psychiatrist Dr. Drew Ramsey discusses how poor diets and a lack of nutrients have harmed our brains, causing anxiety and depression and why a client who visits him now for problems with her love life might just leave his office with a bunch of kale! [22]

His best-seller Books: "The Happiness Diet" and "Fifty Shades of Kale" are expounding the virtues of the right kind of nutrition supporting brain health. [23]

The scary truth which has been observed in Dr. Ramsey's clinic is that the modern brain is shrinking!

Conversely, if we pay attention to specific nutrient rich foods, our brain grows.

Our lifestyle creates a state of inflammation in the brain. It seems that several patients who struggle with resistant depression are also struggling with chronic inflammation. There is also data showing that if you add an anti-inflammatory onto antidepressant treatments you can double the efficacy of how well that antidepressant works. This begs the question: "Do depressed people have inflamed brains?"

Science is finally making the connection between food and health of the brain, where brain health and body health are inextricably tied together.

Nutritional Psychiatry is relatively new but making rapid inroads into psychiatric clinics. [24]

The interest in Neuro-Inflammation has engendered a new science about brain health: BDNF – "Brain-derived-neurotropic-factor" which is focused on helping brain cells to regenerate themselves.

Data suggests that BDNF increases with a healthy diet. [25]

The New Science of Nutritional Psychiatry

Brain food prescription as recommended by Dr. Drew Ramsay [26] [27]

- Zinc. Magnesium, omega-3 fats (building blocks of the cells of the brain)
- Magnesium in kale and dark chocolate
- Vit B12: Curry curcumin, green tea, onion, dark chocolate
- Vit E: Almonds

- Vit B and folate, to make serotonin and dopamine: red bean and lentils: top antioxidant foods and source of folate

- Nutrient density is most important – ex: Zinc: pumpkin seeds, oysters – 6x oysters cover 500% of nutrient daily needs

- Long chain omega fats in wild salmon, anchovies, oysters, clams, mussels

- Iron: Your IQ can go up by 13 %

- **Superfood Kale:**

  Kale helps build healthy bacteria and your gut is in constant contact with your brain.

  Kale is also a nutrient dense food: it has Vit K. One cup of raw kale = 204% of vit A recommended dose! Half cup of kale contains 33 calories and provides 608% of the daily recommended intake of vitamin K, which is an essential fat-soluble vitamin necessary for maintaining a healthy brain."

  Kale offers the equivalent of 134% Vit c = 100s of phytonutrients and is a more absorbable calcium than a glass of milk.

Best Nootropics and Superfoods for Brain Health

What if ingesting a supplement or herb could increase your cognitive abilities and help you think better? This is the promise of nootropics, or "smart drugs", which are becoming increasingly popular as executives are looking for ways to improve their mental performance. There is much information available on various sites and in many publications. The best summary for these amazing nootropics has been published by Ari Whitten M.S. He is a natural health expert who takes an evidence-based approach to human energy optimization and has some powerful recommendations in his published research "The Energy Blueprint". [28]

These supplements work through a variety of mechanisms, such as increasing blood flow to the brain, providing essential nutrients, improving neurotransmitter function, reducing inflammation in the brain and providing antioxidant protection. By taking some of these supplements, super herbs and superfoods regularly, you can help your brain stay healthy and functioning at optimum level. Here are a few suggestions for you to choose from that offer simplicity, availability and ease of use when incorporating them into your diet. [29]

List for Best Nootropics and Superfoods for Brain Health

- **Rhodiola Rosea:** enhancing mental performance and resilience to stress
- **Lion's Mane Powder:** Medicinal Mushroom; cognitive-enhancing, neuroprotective and mood stabilizing properties
- **Vitamin E:** significantly increases concentration and prevents brain damage and neurotoxicity
- **Magnesium:** essential for mitochondrial health and required for optimal nerve transmission and protection against neurotoxicity
- **Brahmi – (Bacopa Monnieri):** traditionally used in Ayurvedic medicine for the enhancement of memory and cognition, as well as a general brain tonic
- **Ginkgo Biloba:** Herb: neuroprotective, antioxidant, preserves brain receptors from ageing, counteracts cognitive impairment, enhances neuronal plasticity and improves memory
- **Coffee:** powerful antioxidant compounds that benefit our brain
- **Yuan Zhi (Polygala Tenuifolia):** used in traditional Chinese medicine – Root; for depression and used to improve memory and combat forgetfulness with ageing
- **Ashwagandha - (Withania Somnifera):** evergreen shrub known as Indian Ginseng: revered in Ayurvedic medicine for its physical and mental enhancing effects; increases a person's resilience to stress and helps reduce anxiety
- **Dopamine Boosters:** 2 recommendations: Mucuna Pruriens = Velvet Bean and Tyrosine.
- **Acetylcholine Boosters:** involved in regulating muscle contractions of the heart, blood vessels, and skeletal muscle, as well as the ability to learn and remember. Three recommendations: Alpha-GPC: improves cognition - CDP-choline: for memory enhancement - Huperzine-A: for cognition improvement
- **GABA Boosters:** to reduce distraction in the brain
- **Serotonin Boosters:** Serotonin modulates mood, perception, reward, anger, aggression, appetite, memory and attention. Two recommendations: 5-HTP for mood enhancement and Saffron, a medicinal and culinary spice. Ancient Persians used saffron to treat depression and modern research has since supported this use with additional antioxidant benefits and neuroinflammation reduction

> **"In modern times, Lion's Mane has become famed for its nootropic effects, aiding the brain's plasticity and capacity to function, as well as supporting nervous system regulation. Read on to learn the 6 reasons you should be taking Lion's Mane for your brain!"**
>
> - Mason Tailor and Madison Crothers – Superfeast

Food for Thoughts

- Your brain consumes 20/30% of the calories you consume

- Your brain requires the most resources above any other organ

- Human brain is the hungriest organ in your body

- It is electric!

- Human brain can grow

- Your brain is the organ of connection

- Your brain is a Universe of possibilities inside you

- Healthy brain sleeps better, learns better, smiles more, finds love and falls in love

SUMMARY OF CHAPTER SIX
The Brain and Epigenetics - Mitochondria -Psychiatry

- The Brain and Epigenetics – Mitochondria - Psychiatry
  - o The science of epigenetics - Genus versus the environment
  - o You can control your cells environment
  - o Major obstacle 1 - Sugar
  - o Major obstacle 2 – Gluten
  - o Major obstacle 3 - Toxins
  - o Reprogram your future with epigenetics with the world's top anti-ageing specialist
  - o 90 Anti inflammation foods   A-Z chart
- The Brain and Mitochondria
  - o Importance of the mitochondria for the brain
  - o A story of brain redemption
  - o Food plan for mitochondria and your brain
- Vegetable Kingdom - daily
- Animal Kingdom – weekly
- Ocean Kingdom - Weekly
  - o Supplements for Mitochondria Health
  - o Foods to avoid
  - o 20 Superfoods for your brain and mitochondria
- The brain and Psychiatry: Lack of Nutrients causing brain damage.
  - o The new science of Nutritional Psychiatry
- Best Nootropics and Superfoods for Brain Health
- Food for thoughts

CHAPTER SEVEN

Stem Cells Support

"Immortalised throughout Chinese art, temples, statues, and paintings, Reishi mushroom was held in the highest esteem amongst Chinese royalty and is surrounded by many legends over the past 4 millennia. She came to be the supreme protector, the Queen of the mushrooms."

Terry Willard, Herbalist

CHAPTER SEVEN

Stem Cells Support

- **The Three Treasures for Longevity**
- **Superfoods and Medicinal Mushrooms**
- **AFA – Blue Green Algae – Phytoplankton**
- **Fasting**

Medicine Around the World and the Mind-Body Connection

For millennia across the globe, many cultures have sought the fountain of youth. The ancient Vedic sages spoke of a special procedure called Kaya Kalpa, which restores an aged body to youthful vigour. Ancient Chinese, Hebrew and Egyptian sages reportedly knew how to live far longer than modern man, and anti-ageing herbs were commonly used.

In Chinese medicine the three treasures are the basis of health, vigour, energy and vitality.

The Three Treasures: Jing, Qi and Shen – are substances/energies that we cultivate in qigong and Inner Alchemy practice. Though there is no exact English translation for Jing, Qi and Shen, they are often translated as Essence, Vitality and Spirit.

The three Treasures

1- Jing in the Lower Dantian – Kidney

The most concentrated or densely vibrating energy is Jing.

Of the Three Treasures, Jing is the one associated most closely with our physical body.

The home of Jing is the **lower dantian** or the **Kidney** Organ System and the reproductive energy of the sperm and ova.

Jing is the root of our Vitality, the physical substance out of which our life unfolds, the physical basis for our functioning system.

Jing is lost through excessive stress or worry.

It is also depleted in younger men and women via excessive sexual activity and heavy menstruation.

The good news is that Jing can be restored through dietary and herbal supplements, as well as through qigong practice. (Similar to Tai Chi).

Jing emphasizes the importance of nurturing relationships, cultivating harmony and promoting mutual respect. By nurturing Jing we can foster understanding between people from different backgrounds and cultures, which can lead to greater collaboration and cooperation. Nurturing Jing is essential for creating a harmonious society that values diversity and inclusion where everyone feels respected and valued.

There are specific super-herbs that you can incorporate in your diet to support a healthy Jing, specifically in the mushroom kingdom with Reishi, Cordyceps and Turkey Tail. [1] HeShuWu is also a top adaptogen super herb used as a Jing tonic, as well as Lycium Barbarum (Goji Berries) and Schizandra berries. [2]

2- Qi in the Middle Dantian - Liver

Qi – life-force energy – is that which animates our bodies, which allows movement of all sorts: the movement of breath in and out of our lungs, the movement of blood through the vessels, the functioning of the various Organ Systems, etc.

The home of Qi is the **middle dantian**, and it is associated with the **Liver and Spleen** Organ Systems.

Qi deficiency is believed to be at the root of many common Western disorders, such as chronic fatigue syndrome, diabetes, indigestion, menstrual cramps, general weakness, heart palpitations, memory loss, hair loss, anxiety, mental fog. [3]

It is believed that by nurturing Qi, one can achieve physical and mental balance. This balance leads to increased energy levels, and a greater sense of wellbeing.

There are simple steps that you can take to regulate your Qi by getting sufficient restful sleep, exercising regularly with focus on your breath, maintaining healthy eating habits and taking care of your mental health.

There are specific Chinese herbs used for supporting Qi such as Astragalus, Ginseng, Rhodiola [2]

3- Shen in the Upper Dantian - Heart

The third of the Three Treasures is Shen, which is our Spirit or Mind (in its largest sense).

The home of Shen is the **upper dantian**, and it is associated with the **Heart** Organ System.

Shen is the spiritual radiance that can be seen shining through a person's eyes – the emanation of a universal loving-kindness, compassion and enlightened power of a heart brimming with wisdom, forgiveness and generosity.

The Three Treasures bear a similarity to the Western Mind-Body-Spirit connection.

Nurturing these three centres has been known to support good health and longevity.

Reishi mushroom tonifies all the three treasures as does Astragalus root. (2)

Chinese Herbs, Medicinal Mushrooms and Stem Cell Support
Ancient wisdom and Elixir of life

Stem cells have unique abilities to self-renew and to recreate functional tissues.

Given their unique regenerative abilities, there are many ways in which human stem cells are being used in biomedical research and development of therapeutics. (4) (5) (6)

Chinese herbs, medicinal mushrooms and natural stem cell support are becoming increasingly popular as natural remedies for a variety of health issues and they are also being studied for their potential to help with cancer treatment and other diseases.

These natural remedies offer many benefits including improved immunity, better digestion, increased energy levels, inflammation reduction and improved mental clarity. By combining the power of these herbs, mushrooms and stem cells with modern science, we can create powerful treatments to support executive functions in the workforce and generally to live healthier, happier lives. (7) (8)

1- Reishi, the mushroom of Immortality [9] [10] [11] [12] [13]

Reishi mushrooms (Ganoderma lucidum) have been used for medicinal purposes for at least 2,000 years. The mushrooms were known to the ancients as "the mushroom of immortality" for good reason. They had the reputation of promoting health and longevity, boosting the immune system and reducing the risk of life-shortening conditions such as cardiovascular disease and cancer.

Science has finally validated this traditional wisdom. There is now a wealth of impressive data that demonstrates Reishi's life extending properties but also its significant ability to stimulate brain neurons, search and destroy cancer cells and prevent the development of new fat cells in obese individuals.

Research with lab mice has also shown a life span extension of 9% to 20% —the equivalent of 7 to 16 years in human terms.

Reishi's numerous compounds show a therapeutic effect on asthma, allergies, autoimmune diseases, Alzheimer's and Parkinson's diseases, diabetes, liver disease and more.

2- Turkey Tail Mushroom for Inner Health [9] [10] [11] [12]

Turkey tail mushroom (Trametes versicolor) is another powerful fungi!

It has been used for thousands of years in Traditional Chinese Medicine (TCM) to support health and general wellbeing. It may assist with antioxidant benefits as well as liver and immune system support. These mushrooms have successfully been used for centuries to help restore, protect and build the body's inner health.

114

- Enhances and supports the immune system
- Antioxidant
- Promotes stamina and endurance
- Aids in the improvement of general wellbeing

3- Shiitake Mushroom, the "Miracle Mushroom" [9] [10] [11] [12]

Shiitake (Lentinula edodes) is prized around the world for its medicinal properties. It is one of the most popular sources of protein in China, Japan and the rest of Asia. Its popularity is not due to its ample protein but its delicious flavour and other medicinal attributes.

A strong antiviral effect is believed to be caused by the number of interferons inherent in the mushroom. Interferons are natural proteins that are typically created in vertebrates which create them as a reaction to viruses, bacteria, cancerous cells and parasites. Boosts the immune system of the consumer.

It lowers blood cholesterol levels by up to 40-45% and is an excellent substitute for cholesterol heavy meats.

Japan has developed an extract from Shiitake known as Lentinan which has become the leading prescription treatment for cancer. Lentinan may also prevent chromosomal damage induced by anti-cancer drugs.

As a food source, Shiitake contain all eight of the essential amino acids in a better ratio than meat, milk, eggs or soybeans; they contain an excellent combination of vitamins and minerals including A, B, B12, C, and D. In addition, Shiitake produce a fat-absorbing compound which is perfect for those wanting to lose weight. It's no wonder why the Shiitake is also known as the "miracle mushroom".

4- He Shou Wu (fo ti) [9] [10] [11] [12]

He Shou Wu is a powerful Chinese anti-ageing herb for potentially reversing a loss of hair or greying hair, but more importantly, having general anti-ageing and life-extension properties.

He Shou Wu is good to strengthen the muscles and tendons. It is also very beneficial for the nerves. It is used for backaches, knee joint pain, traumatic bruises and neurasthenia. It has been used to lower blood pressure. Many people say it helps them to fall asleep at night.

He Shou Wu is an herb with a long history to support health and rejuvenation. It is a tonic for the endocrine glands and supports stamina and resistance to disease.

5- Cordyceps [9] [10] [11] [12]

Caterpillar mushroom (Cordyceps sinensis) is associated with stamina and longevity.

50,000 years ago in China, only the Imperial family and the powerful and rich had privilege to access Cordyceps sinensis

In 1993, as mentioned in the Encyclopedia Britannica, Cordyceps was used by the Chinese Government for the Beijing Olympics because of its wide range of health benefits and produced 3 gold medals for the Chinese Olympics female running team who broke records for 1,500, 3,000 and 10,000 meters

Cordyceps sinensis increases ATP (adenosine triphosphate) levels in the body by almost 28 per cent. ATP is the body's energy supply source and is required for all enzyme processes.

Some benefits of Cordyceps:

- Regulates the immune function
- Anti-oxidation effect (oxidation is the major process of ageing)
- Anti-inflammatory effect (inflammation is a cause of wide range of health problems)
- Anti-bacterial effect and anti-viral effect
- Anti-tumour effect
- Strengthen the lungs/respiratory system
- Benefits the heart
- Kidney tonic
- Regulates the blood sugar and lipid levels and helps to regenerate red blood cells.
- Powerful overall anti-ageing

6- Astragalus [9] [10] [11] [12]

Astragalus is gentle and easier on sensitive bodies than other mushrooms.

Astragalus is a plant native to Asia. The Chinese name of the herb, Huang Qi, means "yellow leader", because the root is yellow, and it is one of the most important herbs in traditional Chinese medicine. The part of the plant used medicinally is the root.

Immune Function: One of the key uses for astragalus is to improve immune function and has antiviral activity and help with the prevention of colds.

Astragalus is also used for various heart conditions and could lower blood pressure.

Side effects: Whilst Astragalus is an important herb which acts on longevity pathways, it is better to consult with a medical practitioner familiar with Chinese medicinal herbs prior to ingesting it.

7- Lion's Mane [14]

Lion's Mane is renowned for its brain and gut protection properties.

Lion's mane (*Hericium erinaceus*) is a wonder mushroom used for thousands of years by traditional herbalists to boost digestive health and in recent times has become famous as a nootropic, supporting the brain's plasticity and function. It also supports the regulation of the nervous system.

Lion's Mane helps with gastrointestinal challenges and supports the creation of a healthy gut lining. It is also suggested as a great tonic for the immune system.

It has been used for a long time in traditional Chinese medicine with claims to benefit a wide range of health imbalances from cancer prevention to boosting energy, weight loss and improving symptoms of depression. Most of the reported benefits are related to neuroprotective benefits. [15]

Lion's Mane can play a role in stroke recovery and may be a potential alternative medicine for the treatment of depression. Several in vitro (test tube) studies have suggested that polysaccharides in Lion's Mane may protect neurons or make them function better. [17]

Improving memory: Lion's mane mushrooms may double neuron growth. [18]

Lion's Mane is recommended for:

- Brain Cognition [16]
- Digestive Health
- Healthy Stress Response
- Immunity
- Long Term Neurological Health
- Memory & Recall

Natural Stem Cell Support – AFA – Blue Green Algae [19]

AFA – Blue Green Algae supports synergistic stem cell release:

AFA (aphanizonenon flos-aqua) or Blue Green algae is found to grow prolifically in Lake Klamath and is scientifically documented to stimulate the migration of adult stem cells from the bone marrow into the bloodstream.

Microalgae phytoplankton forms the basis of the food chain.

Microalgae are responsible for an estimated 80 to 90 percent of the planet's overall food supply and oxygen supply.

AFA is a nitrogen-fixing algae that draws nitrogen from the atmosphere to build world-class protein.

Blue-green algae is a wild food with a fantastic array of brain-specific phytochemicals, a huge selection of antioxidants, minerals (especially iron, zinc, selenium and magnesium), amino acids (it is a complete protein), vitamins, enzymes and many unique nutrients. Blue-green algae is one of the richest food sources of antioxidant compounds including carotenoids (beta carotene, lycopene and lutein), chlorophyll and phycocyanin.

The antioxidant phycocyanin is a pigment that provides the intense blue colour in blue-green algae. It provides a range of health benefits some of which fight chronic inflammation, support the liver, protect against free-radical damage, improve the production of neurotransmitters and aid production of rejuvenating stem cells.

Phenylethylamine (PEA) is also found in the AFA. PEA is an adrenal and brain chemical which elevates dopamine levels increasing mental concentration and feelings of joy.

Iron: AFA algae is exceptionally rich in bioavailable iron.

Raw DNA and RNA from AFA algae assembles new genetically healthy cells and rejuvenates damaged cells and tissues.

Digestive Wellness: Raw algae, honey and grasses (e.g., wheatgrass juice) are some of the richest sources of enzymes contributing to our digestive wellness. [20][21]

Carotenoids: AFA algae are extraordinarily rich in carotenoids such as beta-carotene. Research continues to demonstrate that the greater the beta-carotene content of one's diet, the longer one lives.

Al Glutamine one of the main amino acids in marine phytoplankton and after glucose the most useable energy source, so it can go right into the cell and produce ATP energy. [22]

It is a glyconutrient, which is crucial to life.

AFA acts on the immune and nervous systems and prevents inflammation. [23]

AFA contains alpha-linolenic acid (ALA) and the long-chain omega-3 fatty acid known as docosahexanoic acid (DHA), promotes wellness and rejuvenation. [24] [25]

Undaria Pinnatifida, a marine algae is known to support the immune system and supports a long-lasting increase in the number of circulating stem cells.

Integrating stem cell support with other superfoods daily offers full spectrum minerals, providing complete nutrition to the cells and boosting your brain health to the highest level. [26]

In summary – Phytoplanktons are the fastest way to deliver nutrients directly to the brain.

If you want to have the life experience of feeling great and functioning at optimum level, it is what stem cells do for you, which is what healthy brain cells do. If the central command system, the brain, is working well, the rest of the body can be monitored and works much more efficiently.

So, focusing on the brain is the main aim because the brain knows how to do all those things it needs to do to repair itself and to maintain a healthy operating system.

It is the brain that tells the body to release the stem cells.

Marine phytoplankton is a primordial food, by far the best for the human body to consume, it has all the required elements in it.

Of course, we need a variety of foods, because they each fulfil a particular function, but if there was a choice – marine phytoplankton covers every single base, covering every nutritional gap.

With all food you ingest, always ask yourself: How effective is it for my brain?

If it is good for the brain, it is good for the heart, good for the nervous system, good for every part of the system, immune, endocrine - because it provides every nutrient needed and every essential fatty acid.

> ## Fasting is just a word. Eat Less and Live longer..
>
> ### Dr Valter Longo

Phytoplankton's pass the blood-brain barrier and enter the cells of the brain effectively without needing the liver to process them; it is instantly utilisable! [27]

Fasting to Activate Stem Cell Regeneration

Dr. Valter Longo [28] is a biogerontologist and cell biologist known for his studies on the role of fasting and nutrient response genes on cellular protection ageing and diseases. [29]

In his book "The Longevity Diet", Dr. Valter presents his clinically proven applied studies where his fasting-mimicking diets have revolutionized research on stem cells' regeneration and longevity promotion. [30]

Fasting is an ancient practice that has been used for centuries to improve health and longevity. In recent years, scientific research has revealed the powerful biological effects of fasting, including its ability to reset your body's metabolism, boost your immune system and even extend your lifespan. Both Dr. Longo and David Asprey's research, among others, have proven that fasting can reset your biology and support your longevity. [31]

Dr. Longo's research presents an easy way to fasting with his 5 Day Fasting Mimicking diet, which only needs to be done 3 to 4 times a year to achieve the same age beneficial health effects.

His clinically proven diet can activate stem cells and promote regeneration and rejuvenation in multiple organs to reduce the risk for diabetes, cancer, Alzheimer's and heart disease.

Overall, he suggests a vegan diet with a little fish 2 to 3 times a week.

His 5-day mimicking diet is essentially a calorie reduced diet of 800 to 1,100 calories/day for five days.

He further suggests confining eating within a 12-hour period - say between 8am and 8pm and ideally with no food intake for at least 3 hours before bedtime.

Integrating stem cell support with superfoods daily THE BEST Smoothy on the planet!	
Coconut water: 1 cup	Super hydration, reduce BP, Nutrients rich, tighten skin, keep slim
Celery sticks: 1 cup	Alkalise, reduce inflammation, aids digestion, good for eyes, lower BP
Mint: few springs	Highest antioxidants, aids digestion, treatment for IBS, Excellent skin
Parsley: few sprigs	Super high in Vit K, high in C, healthy heart, protect rheumatoid arthritis
Kale: 1 cup	Detox, Iron, vit K, Vit c, calcium, anti-inflammatory, cardiovascular support
1 Apple (1 piece of fruit)	Protect against Alzheimer, Parkinson's, cancer, reduce cholesterol
Coconut oil: 2 tablespoons	Brain health, antihistamines, anti-infectives/antiseptics, promoter of immunity, nontoxic anticancer agents, anti-ageing, lower cholesterol, boost metabolism, promote weight loss, improve heart health, boost thyroid
Green Blue Algae: 10 drops	High protein, boost immune system, natural anti-viral properties, relieve fatigue, lower blood cholesterol levels, reduce blood pressure, stem cell support
He Shou Wu: ½ teaspoon	Endocrine tonic, stamina, resistance to disease reduce cholesterol, promote red blood cells, rid intestinal parasite, improve cardiovascular system, anti-ageing, antioxidant, enhance immune function, stem cell support
Hemp Protein: 1 tablespoon	Contain all the 21 known amino acids = fuel that muscles burn for energy

www.TheAgelessExecutive.com

SUMMARY OF CHAPTER SEVEN

Stem Cells Support & Superfoods

The Three Treasures and Fasting

Superfoods and Medicinal Mushrooms

AFA – Blue Green Algae – Phytoplankton

- Medicine around the world
- Chinese Medicine and the Mind-Body Connection – the three treasures

    Jing – Kidneys

    Qi - Liver

    Shen - Heart

- Chinese Herbs and Stem Cell Support. - Ancient wisdom and Elixir of life

    Reishi - The Mushroom of Immortality

    Turkey Tail Mushroom for Inner Heath

    Shiitake Mushroom – The Miracle Mushroom

    He Shou Wu – Rejuvenation

    Cordyceps – Stamina and Longevity

    Astragalus - Heart

    Lion's Mane – Brain Power

- Natural stem cell support – AFA – Blue Green Algae
- Fasting to activate Stem Cell Regeneration
- The best smoothy on the planet!

CHAPTER EIGHT

Stress Management and Meditation

"Meditation is not a way of making the mind go quiet. It's a way of entering into the quiet that's already there – buried under the 50,000 thoughts, the average person thinks every day."

Deepak Chopra

CHAPTER EIGHT

Stress Management and Meditation

Stress: The Real Epidemic

No one escapes stressful experiences. Thankfully, our bodies are built to handle most circumstances and we sometimes even thrive and grow from these, but not all the time. Indeed, our health can become seriously affected after going through long periods of stress.

Science shows that we can develop autoimmune disorders from three types of stresses: daily stressors of modern life, a major stressful event or emotional trauma from childhood.

Physiologically, our bodies react with chemical reactions such as hormonal releases from the adrenal glands, cortisol, epinephrine/adrenaline and norepinephrine, which are released into the bloodstream and prepare our bodies to either fight or to run.

When this occurs, the sympathetic nervous system is activated, triggering both heart rate and blood pressure increases. Your muscles will also tighten and digestion will stop.

When the real or imaginary threat is removed or released, your body will return to the control of the parasympathetic nervous system and relax, returning to normal bodily functions.

However, what happens when you do not go back to a relaxation response?

Studies have shown that every system and every organ is impacted, including impaired immune cells leading to out-of-control inflammation associated with autoimmune disorders.

The main tragedy with stress is that it causes disease and the disease itself causes stress, quite a vicious cycle! [1] [2]

In 2020-21, 3.4 million Australians aged 16-85 years (17%) saw a health professional for their mental health.

How Stress Damages the Brain

Stress, pressure, fatigue, poor diet, alcohol and drugs damage neural connections between the brain's prefrontal cortex—or "CEO"—and the rest of the brain. When you are overtired or under intense mental or physical stress, the brain bypasses its "higher," more evolved rational frontal executive circuits.

The brain then starts using more primitive stimulus/response pathways. Consequently, you respond to daily demands without thinking; you make impulsive, short-sighted decisions.

When the CEO goes "offline," strong emotions such as fear and anger take over, adversely colouring your view of the world. [3]

It is well documented that the pre-frontal cortex of the brain shrinks as we get older, affecting our memory and making it harder for us to make decisions.

BUT the good news is that many studies also show that this can be reversed.

> ## 85% of illness is caused by stress.
>
> ### *(Electric Body) - Eileen McKusic*

Stressed Brain Executive Functions

Aggravated by tension and fatigue

Weak Executive Functioning	Stressed Physiology	Imbalanced Emotions
Tendency towards	*Tendency towards*	*Tendency towards*
Rigid Thinking	Fatigue	Low self-esteem and self confidence
Impulsive, reactive behaviour	High blood pressure	Worries, anxieties and fears
Short-sighted decision-making	Eating and sleeping disorders	Shallow, divisive emotions
Poor working memory	Weak immune system	Unstable relationships
Distracted attention		Depression
Drug and alcohol abuse		
Unethical thinking and behaviour		

In one of Deepak Chopra's discourses he made the following statement:

"We have 65,000 thoughts/day and 98% of those thoughts we had yesterday.

So, if there is a mind trip with this, or anxiety or overwhelm or fear, etc … get back to the present by using the breath and stay with the purity of the sensation, without interpretation.

Detach yourself from what is happening. Look at it, then act, so that you are not connected to what the mind wants to do.

That situation can change in 12 seconds-

Kids and animals always live in the present; that is why it is easy for them to be authentic.

When we change our thoughts, we can change our reality."

Reducing Stress to Decrease Autoimmune Disease

A study at Massachusetts General Hospital confirms that relaxation-response techniques like meditation, yoga and prayer, could reduce the need for health care services by 43 percent. [4]

Imagine how simple relaxation practices might reduce or eliminate your need for medication whilst still allowing you to operate at peak performance level in your executive position!

Fortunately, there are several scientifically proven strategies that can help reduce stress and are relatively simple to adopt.

- **A good night's sleep.**

Sleep is one of the most important activities for our bodies and minds. It is essential for our physical and mental health as well as our overall well-being. Unfortunately, many of us do not get enough sleep or prioritize it correctly.

Chronic sleep deprivation can lead to a range of health issues such as cardiovascular disease, diabetes, obesity, cancer, and can affect your longevity. [5]

Science is unearthing more and more information on the role of sleep, its importance and the consequences of not getting enough sleep. So much so that I have dedicated a whole chapter to the subject. (Chapter Ten)

- **Deep conscious breath**

Slow, controlled belly breathing calms the brain's arousal centre, activates the calming rest-and-digest parasympathetic nervous system, and sends the message to your mind and body that all is well. Repeat 6 times.

This simple technique has proven to significantly increase feelings of relaxation and increase heartrate variability, an important indicator of health, resilience and youthfulness. [6]

- **Keep Moving**

Sitting for long periods of time has been linked to a variety of health issues, including obesity, diabetes, heart disease and even cancer. Recent studies have shown that sitting for more than four hours per day can increase the risk of developing these conditions. This is especially true when combined with a lack of physical activity. [7]

Exercise is an important part of a healthy lifestyle. It not only helps to keep our bodies fit and strong, but it also has many other benefits. Consistent exercise such as 30 minutes of walking, cycling, swimming or strength training can help reduce inflammation in the body and enhance the immune system. It can also help to reduce stress levels and improve overall mental health. [8]

- **Time in Nature**

Research seems to indicate that spending most of your time indoors can lead to health issues, whereas spending time in nature offers outstanding health benefits such as lowered cortisol, reduced inflammation, improved immune function, decreased feelings of

depression and anxiety and even improved memory. (9)

Make sure you get outside and spend time with mother nature! (10)

The benefits are immeasurable, and it is well-known that a little sun will increase your vitamin D levels, improve your mood and your sleep. (11)

• **Forgiveness**

According to Dr. Steven Standiford, chief of surgery at the Cancer Treatment Centres of America, unforgiveness, classified in medical books as a disease, makes people sick and keeps them that way. Forgiveness therapy is now being used to help treat diseases such as cancer.

Dr. Karen Swartz stated that forgiveness can lead to huge health rewards, lowering the risk of heart attack, improving cholesterol levels and sleep, reducing pain anxiety, depression and stress. (12)

It is all about a conscious, deliberate decision to release feelings of resentment or vengeance toward a person or group who has harmed you, regardless of whether they deserve your forgiveness.

The practice of a short and effective Hawaiian prayer called Ho'oponopono has proven very effective with the inspiring story of Dr. Hew Len as narrated by Joe Vitale in his book "Point Zero", where Dr. Len worked with this prayer and healed and cleared a ward of mentally ill criminals. Their health improved and within a very short period were healed and healthy and released back into society. That ward was subsequently closed.

What is important to understand about this is that the prayer is not about correcting or healing anyone outside of the self. It is about forgiving oneself for one's own perceptions and feelings.

133

Self-forgiveness is very powerful, reducing the risk of clinical depression and improving health by lowering markers of inflammation. [13]

This practice is very simple: when thinking about people who have harmed you, just say this prayer a few times: **Ho'oponopono: I'm sorry. Please forgive me. Thank you. I love you.**

Science is also definite about the benefits of meditation which has shown to decrease stress, anxiety, depression, increase resilience and empathy, increase the size of your brain and produce beneficial and immediate changes in the expression of genes involved in immune function. [14] [15]

What REALLY is Meditation?

Meditation is simply the progressive quieting of the mind until it reaches a place of total stillness.

In spiritual traditions, this place of total stillness is the realm of the spirit.

It was originally developed to transcend the mind and give a spiritual experience.

The past 30 years, meditation has been used as a means for stress management. [16]

As mentioned earlier, the mind and body are inseparable - any changes in one will affect the other.

Meditation can reverse the stress response.

Over the last 30 years there have been over 800 publications in scientific literature peer-reviewed journals that show that not only does meditation lower stress but it also lowers the risk for heart disease, infections and even accidents.

When you learn to meditate and practice meditation you will begin to realize that meditation is more than stress management.

Progressive awakening and expansion of consciousness results in more insight, more intuition, more conscious choice making, even more imagination and creativity.

Getting in touch with the essential YOU.

Google Endorsed Meditation

In Silicon Valley, major companies including Google, Facebook and Twitter have adopted mindfulness practices. [17] [18] [19]

Neuroscience and Meditation

Neuroscience and evolutionary biology are two interrelated fields of study that have been gaining more attention in recent years. Neuroscience focuses on the structure and function of the nervous system, while evolutionary biology studies how species change over time. Together, these two disciplines provide a comprehensive understanding of how humans and other organisms interact with their environment. By studying both neuroscience and evolutionary biology, we can gain insight into how our brains work, why certain behaviours are adaptive. [20]

The amygdala, the region of the brain believed to be responsible for processing fear, can override the rest of the mind's ability to think logically.

Meditation can rewire how the brain responds to stress. Research suggests that meditation improves working memory and executive function. Several studies by long-term practitioners show an increased ability to concentrate on fast-changing stimuli. [21] [22]

Meditation has been proven to have a positive effect on the immune system. [23]

Cultivating emotional intelligence: emotionally connected employees tend to remain at their current workplaces; a great tool for employee retention. [24]

It is hard to focus in our "always-on" culture, but luckily the neuroscience of mindfulness has shown that it is possible to increase our ability to focus with a practice of meditation. [25]

Develop Your Total Brain with Meditation for Executive Peak Performance!

Case studies about *preventing and solving* executive issues. [26][27][28]	Immediate and longer-term *benefits*
Executive burnout	Greater relaxation (I) Emotional mastery (LT)
Anxiety and depression	Dissolve stress, worry and anxiety, improvement in mood(I) Greater inner peace and serenity LT)
Poor planning and decision-making	Increased focus levels, enhanced creativity(I) Enhanced creativity (LT)
Memory loss	Increased brain power (LT)
Drug and alcohol abuse	Dozens of proven health benefits (LT)
High blood pressure	Dozens of proven health benefits (LT)
Sleep disorders	Dozens of proven health benefits (LT)
Health care costs	Dozens of proven health benefits (LT)
Scattered mind	Focused mind

Corporate Leadership through the Transcendental Meditation Program [29]

Supported by a large amount of research, meditation is finally reaching main-stream even in the workplace, where everyone from C-suite executives to entry-level assistants can share in massive amount of benefits such as:

- Developing Your Total Brain for Executive Peak Performance
- Eliminating harmful stress
- Optimizing decision-making and planning
- Improving cardiovascular health
- Improving productivity

Some of these benefits have been documented by 40 years of scientific research and boardroom experience and were presented by the association of professionals practicing the Transcendental Meditation Program.

How Meditation Optimizes the Brain

- Meditation provides the experience of "restful alertness," which reduces stress, strengthens communication between the brain's prefrontal cortex and different areas of the brain and develops total brain functioning.

- As a result, the TM practitioner displays stronger executive functions, with more purposeful thinking and farsighted decision-making. When the CEO is fully "online," the emotional response to the world is more balanced and appropriate.

˰˰˰˰˰˰˰˰˰˰˰˰˰˰˰˰	GAMMA	Active Thought - Most powerful brainwave to date
˰˰˰˰˰˰˰˰˰˰˰˰˰˰˰˰	BETA	Alert, Working
˰˰˰˰˰˰˰˰˰˰˰˰˰˰˰˰	ALPHA	Relaxed Focus, Reflective
˰˰˰˰˰˰˰˰˰˰˰˰˰˰˰˰	THETA	Dreaming, Drowsy, Meditative
˰˰˰˰˰˰˰˰˰˰˰˰˰˰˰˰	DELTA	Sleepy, Dreamless sleep

Coherent Brain Executive Signs

Strong Executive Functioning	Healthy Physiology	Balanced Emotions
Trend towards	*Trend towards*	*Trend towards*
Purposeful, flexible thinking	Energy and vitality	Self-confidence and secure self-esteem
Non-impulsive, proactive behaviour	Fit cardiovascular system	Feelings of safety and peace
Farsighted decision-making	Balanced physiology	Compassion and empathy for others
Excellent working memory	Strong immune functioning	Healthy interpersonal relations
Settled, focused attention	Healthy	Happiness and optimism
No substance abuse or addictions	Healthy	Healthy Emotions
Ethical thinking and behaviour	Healthy	Service to others

Meditation and Reverse-Ageing

Meditation can reduce stress, a major trigger for ageing.

You can reverse your biological age by maintaining a youthful mind by changing your perceptions and escaping the jail of conditioning.

The practice of meditation can reduce stress, increase feelings of wellbeing and benefit overall health. It is of specific use to help increase alertness, relaxation and reflection in "waking" states.

Brain waves in meditation shift through various stages. The most common brain waves in meditation are alpha waves. These alpha brain waves in meditation basically promote changes in the autonomic nervous system that calm it. With continuing practice, meditation will reverse the roles of the sympathetic and parasympathetic nervous systems, which lowers blood pressure and heart rate and lowers the amount of stress hormones in the body, as well as calming the mind. One of these stress hormones is cortisol which has been shown to encourage weight gain when it is elevated over the long term.

The 50-year-old meditator has the same amount of activity in the brain as a 20-year-old. Meditation slows down and can reverse the decline of ageing signs like cognitive functions.

One of the fastest ways to put yourself in an alpha state is by imagining yourself in your favourite place. Even when you are in the boardroom, you can quickly get your mind in the alpha state. It takes a little effort to create that ideal space initially, maybe imagining yourself at the beach, feeling the sand between your toes, hearing the surf, feeling the breeze on your skin, smelling the salty air.

In no time at all it becomes automatic and you can summon that state at will, wherever you are, whenever you wish.

When To Practice

Meditation is one of the most effective methods for creating a major shift in consciousness, create deeper peace, harmony, well-being and change your life!

Meditation is a powerful transformational tool. It will increase your energy and vitality, enable you to shift into a positive state of being at will and prepare you to receive the abundant life you are meant to live. This technique will release you from your mind hyperactivity and teach you to remove stress and confusion and give your mind access to clarity and answers.

When you can raise your vibration into a state of strong, positive, clear coherence, you align the systems in your body to work together and align the energies in your environment to work for you.

- First thing in the morning (which is an ideal way to start the day)
- Last thing at night (to let go of the day and get a good sleep)
- During a break in the day (to de-stress and re-connect with your best self and highest intentions.)

Conscious versus Subconscious

Your conscious mind:

- Makes up 17% of total brain mass
- Thoughts you consistently impress from conscious to non-conscious mind determines the results in your life

Your unconscious mind:

- Responsible for 83% to 97% of brain activity

- Impulses travel at more than 100,000 mph
- Reticular Activation System: 800x faster than the conscious mind; sends signals to the conscious mind
- Believes as totally true every picture or image you send to it

With meditation you can retrain your subconscious mind.

You can recalibrate your responses, your Psycho-Cybernetic mechanism: sensors send back feedback to your nervous system which corrects deviation from your intended goal.

Psycho-Cybernetics is a term coined by Dr. Maxwell Maltz, a plastic surgeon, to describe the process of using the power of the mind to achieve desired goals. It is based on the idea that our minds are like computers and can be programmed to respond in certain ways. By understanding how our minds work and how we can use them to our advantage, we can recalibrate our responses and create positive outcomes in our lives. [30]

What Dr. Maxwell Maltz was alluding to is our subconscious mind and the premise of this chapter is that the fastest ways to "reprogram" the subconscious mind is with meditation.

Three Easy Meditation Techniques:

1- Physical Relaxation in 10 Minutes

Systematically relax all the muscles in your body.

In ten minutes you can relax your whole body. Either sitting or lying down, close your eyes. Begin to breathe deeply in through your nose and out through your mouth. Do this a few times. Focus on your breathing. When you are ready, tighten every muscle in your feet as hard as you can, then immediately relax all those muscles. After a few seconds, clench your calf and shin muscles as tightly as possible and then instantly relax them.

Do this, working your way up your entire body, clenching and releasing your thigh, butt, torso, back, hand (make fists), arm, shoulder, neck, and finally face (scrunch your whole face up) muscles, one group at a time. You are systematically releasing the stress that you're holding in your body. When you are finished, your body will be more relaxed. At this time your heart rate will have slowed, your blood pressure will have come down, and your breathing will have become regular and deep. You should feel almost like you could melt into your chair or bed.

A milder form of this exercise is also a method to get to sleep quickly.

Total relaxation of the body is conducive to healing and rejuvenation.

Edua Potor

2- Visualisation to Heal, Energize and Rejuvenate

Sit in a comfortable position.

Imaging that your body is slowly filling with light, starting from the feet, and slowly moving upwards.

As the light is moving up your body, feel that this light is relaxing the muscles and your mind.

Your body is now full of light. Now imagine that any areas of discomfort or pain in your body is surrounded by a dark shadow.

Now feel that you are directing the light towards any area of the body that is giving you pain or discomfort, represented as a shadow on your body.

Feel that you are sending extra light to this area and as you are shining a loving healing light to that area, the darkness is removed.

Feel that this healing light is now radiating throughout each organ and each cell of your body, right down to the DNA, returning you to health, vitality and engaging your body in rejuvenating itself.

3- Conscious Breathing

Focusing on your breath helps quiet the mind.

The 4-7-8 breathing exercise is like an ancient Indian wellness practice, Pranayama. It is a technique that controls the breath through the 3 phases of inhalation, breath retention and exhalation.

Start by sitting up straight in a comfortable position.

Next, place the tip of your tongue on the ridge of your gums, just behind your upper front teeth.

Expand your diaphragm and slowly inhale through your nose for a count of 4.

Hold your breath for another count of 7.

Open your mouth slightly, keeping your tongue in place, and exhale for a count of 8.

Repeat this cycle four times.

Executives Who Swear by Meditation

CEOs have stressful jobs, and some have taken to intense hobbies to alleviate stress, whilst others practice meditation and say that meditating gives them an edge in the competitive business world. Some have even built it into their company›s culture.

Business leaders are embracing meditation rather than other relaxation methods, as it appears to benefit them more. [31]

Meditation will minimize stress and increase productivity.

Some famous CEOs and celebrities have incorporated meditation in their daily lives: [32]

- Jeff Weiner, CEO of LinkedIn
- William Clay Ford Jr., Executive Chairman of Ford Motor Company
- Marc Benioff, Chairman and CEO of SalesForce
- Arianna Huffington, co-founder of HuffPost and Thrive Global
- Oprah
- Madonna

Best Adaptogens to Stress Less and Get Focused [33]

You can use adaptogens to help your body adapt to biological and psychological stress by making it easier for you to balance your hormonal systems.

Adaptogens help you cope with living in the modern world, including fatigue, stress, sleep, impotence and infertility. They will make you more resilient, give you energy, focus, strength and improve your mood.

Ashwagandha (Withania somnifera) is also known as "Indian ginseng". It is a small shrub with yellow flowers that is native to India and Southeast Asia.

It is one of the most common adaptogens and is used in Ayurvedic practices for all kinds of things, most notably for reducing stress. [34] [35]

Several human studies show that Ashwagandha decreases anxiety, stress, c-reactive protein, and cortisol. It also improves memory and has been researched for treating Alzheimer's patients. [36]

Ashwagandha is best for

- Reducing stress and anxiety
- Decreasing c-reactive protein levels
- Lowering the stress-hormone cortisol
- Improving memory formation
- Aiding with neurodegenerative diseases

Brahmi (Bacopa Monnieri) is a creeper plant mostly used as a cognitive and longevity enhancer and as an adaptogen to help with anxiety and depression. It helps to decrease stress in all regions of the brain. [37]

Research shows it reduces the effects of physiological stress, especially when taken in advance of a challenging event. [38]

Brahmi is best for

- Reducing anxiety and stress
- Relieving symptoms of depression
- Improving cognition
- Reducing free radicals
- Boosting memory
- Protecting against toxic metal overload

Holy basil (Tulsi/Ocimum sanctum)

Holy basil, or Tulsi, is an herb used in Ayurvedic medicine and is traditionally used as an adaptogen, aphrodisiac, liver supporter and for longevity!

Studies show the benefits of using holy basil as a stress and anxiety and an antioxidant. [39] [40] [41]

Holy basil is best for

- Reducing stress and anxiety
- Supporting your liver
- Lowering inflammation
- Building muscle mass and lowering body fat
- Boosting your (or your partner's) libido

Mucuna Pruriens (Dopa Bean) has a high content of L-dopa which is a precursor to the neurotransmitter dopamine. This adaptogen is known for its ability to boost your mood, lower stress, improve mood, reduce anxiety and help you focus. [42]

Adding Mucuna to your diet can be effective at calming the nervous system and reducing anxiety, stress and even depression. [43] [44]

Mucuna is best for

- Increasing dopamine
- Lowering stress
- Boosting mood
- Improving fertility
- Enhancing memory and focus

SUMMARY OF CHAPTER EIGHT
Stress Management and Meditation

- Stress: The Real Epidemic
- How Stress Damages the Brain
- Stressed Brain Executive Functions
- Reducing Stress to decrease Autoimmune disease
- What really is Meditation?
- Google endorsed Meditation
- Neuroscience and Meditation
- Develop your total brain with meditation for executive peak performance
- Corporate Leadership through TM Meditation
- How Meditation Optimizes the Brain
- Brain Waves
- Coherent brain executive signs
- Meditation and Reverse-Ageing
- When to Practice
- Conscious versus Sub-conscious
- Three Easy Meditation Techniques
- Executives who swear by Meditation
- Best Adaptogens to Stress less and Get Focused

CHAPTER NINE

Ageless SKIN - Youthful Appearance

"Beauty invariably relates to Nature - Our bodies are made of the same elements as the earth. When we reconnect with nature, with the foods we eat and what we put on our faces, we will heal ourselves and we will heal the planet."

Edua Potor

CHAPTER NINE

Ageless SKIN - Youthful Appearance

Dr. Zebrowitz's research, published in the journal *Current Direction in Psychological Science*, examined how we form first impressions of other people. By analysing how our brains react to certain faces, she observed the most favourable facial characteristics, one of which is fitness. She said "the more your face looks "fit" (healthy), the more people will judge you as someone who is "likable, intelligent and capable." [1]

Today, there is an immense pressure to look good, as is reflected by global anti-ageing skin care revenue in 2022 accounting for about AUD$60 billion! [2]

Skin beauty reflects our overall health and wellbeing. It is an indicator of how well we are taking care of ourselves, both inside and out. All of us want to have that healthy, vibrant look that comes from having a balanced diet, regular exercise and proper skin care. With the right knowledge and tools we can all achieve the beautiful skin we desire.

Skin Ages as We Age

The skin is the most visible biomarker of ageing with external signs such as thinning of the epidermis due to loss of water and lipid content and other manifestations such as decreased collagen turnover and increased senescence. [3]

Although most research into ageing skin tends to focus on the unwelcome aesthetic aspects, skin deterioration is more than a merely cosmetic problem; it can have a significant impact on quality of life.

What Causes Skin to Age?

Skin ageing is a natural process that affects everyone, but there are many factors that can accelerate the process. From environmental damage to lifestyle choices, there is a long list of skin ageing causations that can lead to premature wrinkles and sagging skin.

• Ultraviolet radiation (UVR) • Environmental pollutants • Poor nutrition • Certain personal care products • Carcinogen exposure (e.g., cigarette smoke and alcohol) • Poor sleep • Oestrogen/testosterone decline • Oxidative stress • Accelerated cellular senescence • Gastrointestinal dysbiosis and increased intestinal permeability (IP) • Poor blood glucose control • Muscular atrophy

Intrinsic vs Extrinsic Ageing
Inevitable vs Controllable

The skin is the largest organ of the body, and it is constantly exposed to the outer environment. As a result, it is prone to both intrinsic and extrinsic ageing factors. Intrinsic ageing factors are those that are caused by natural processes such as hormonal changes, while extrinsic ageing factors are those that are caused by external elements such as sun exposure, smoking and pollution. These two types of ageing can cause wrinkles, age spots, sagging skin and other signs of premature ageing.

Intrinsic ageing is a natural process that affects us all, and it is estimated to be responsible for only 3% of the ageing process. On the other hand, extrinsic ageing is a modifiable cause that can be easily rectified and accounts for 97% of the ageing process. This means that we have more control over how we age than we may think. By making simple lifestyle changes such as eating a healthy diet, exercising regularly and avoiding smoking and excessive sun exposure, we can reduce our risk of premature ageing. [4] What specifically influences the health of our skin and what are the specific steps you can take to keep your skin looking youthful?

The Connection of The Ageing Gut with Inflammation and Ageing Skin

When your gut microbiome is out of balance, the cells of the gut do not work properly which causes inflammatory molecules to escape and enter the bloodstream. These molecules get to the skin where they trigger inflammation that causes accelerated ageing or flares of various skin issues. [5]

The microbiome directly impacts ageing through the gastrointestinal system and probiotics and prebiotics may be effective alternatives, considering the relationship between the microbiome and healthy ageing. [6]

Senolytics a New Class of Drugs

Senolytics are a new class of drugs that have the potential to revolutionize the way we treat age-related diseases. These drugs selectively target and kill senescent cells, which are cells that have stopped dividing and can accumulate in our bodies as we age. By eliminating these cells, senolytics can help reduce inflammation, improve tissue function and slow down the ageing process. This would have a tremendous impact on quality of life and the burden of age-related chronic diseases. [7]

Recent studies have shown that dasatinib (D) and quercetin (Q) may be effective in clearing senescent cells. In a study of 46 agents tested in vitro, D and Q showed the most promise in clearing senescent cells.

Senolytics decrease SASP and alter the microbiome. (SASP = senescence-associated secretory phenotype = age associated diseases) [8][9]

- **Quercetin Reduces Senescence Factors in Skin**

Quercetin is a plant flavonol from the flavonoid group of polyphenols. It is found in many fruits, vegetables, leaves, seeds and grains; capers, red onions and kale [10]

Quercetin, a naturally occurring anti-ageing product, has anti-ageing and antioxidant properties that influence cellular lifespan, survival and viability and observed to have a rejuvenating effect. [11]

- **Beta Glucans Support Skin Health**

β-Glucans are found in yeast, fungi (including mushrooms), some bacteria, seaweeds and cereals. Natural β-glucans offer many health benefits such as anticancer, antidiabetic, anti-inflammatory and immune-modulating effects. β-Glucans have shown to have antioxidant activity, anti-wrinkle activity, anti-ultraviolet light, wound healing and moisturizing effect and skin permeation absorption. [12]

Research has shown that β-glucans has a significant impact on the gut microbiota changes and in turn on human health. [13]

- **Zinc Protects the Gut, Skin, and Immune System**

Zinc promotes cell division, cell repair, cell growth and the production of white blood cells. This mineral is essential for cleansing the liver, repairing tissue, and oxygenating the body.

A zinc deficiency is directly linked to acne, hair loss and other skin disorders.

o   Essential for effective wound healing

o   Protects against UV radiation

o   Maintains intestinal barrier function

o   Improves microbial diversity

o   Required for mucin secretion

o   Fundamental to immune cell function

o   Antioxidant [14]

- **Lactobacillus Reuteri (Probiotic) and Skin Rejuvenation**

Lactobacillus reuteri is a probiotic bacterium that has been found to have a positive effect on the skin. Studies have shown that it can reduce the loss of epidermal moisture, which is essential for healthy skin. This probiotic has also been found to reduce inflammation and improve skin barrier function. [15] Additionally, Lactobacillus reuteri can help protect against environmental damage and UV radiation, and has also shown to increase skin thickness, a thicker, shinier hair, mimicking peak health and presenting "youthing" characteristics. [16]

NUTRIENT	WFPB (Whole-Food, Plant-Based) [17] Foods containing Highest Nutrient Concentration	Examples WFPB Foods	Benefits
Vitamin E	Nuts, seeds, some oils, green leafy vegetables	Wheat germ, sunflower seeds, almonds, spinach, kiwifruit, mango, tomatoes	Vit E to reduce in inflammatory skin disorders
Vitamin C	Citrus fruits and vegetables	Red pepper, orange, grapefruit, kiwifruit, green pepper, broccoli, strawberries, tomatoes, cantaloupe, potatoes	Vit C essential for skin regeneration – Collagen production - Wound healing - Reduces melanogenesis – increases immune function [18]
Vitamin A	Leafy green, orange, and yellow vegetables and some fruits	Carrots, broccoli, cantaloupe, squash, tomato	Vit A regulates skin microbiome and immunity. Prevents premature ageing, nourish the skin, and prevent dry skin [19]
Chlorophyll	Green vegetables	Kale, spinach	Can help repair sun damage and heal acne
procyanidin B-2	Apples: Especially Red Delicious and Granny Smith		Skin elasticity - Protects from UV rays. Promotes hair growth - prevents cell damage

Foods that Improve your Appearance from the Inside Out

For Supple Skin

- Water and water rich fruits and vegetables
- Organic apple cider vinegar:
  - Excellent for your digestive system: mix a teaspoon to a tablespoon in your juice
  - Helps your body process sugar and fat which helps in weight control
  - Skin Elasticity
  - Helps shed dead skin
  - Organic apple cider vinegar is the optimum choice

Preventing Wrinkles

- Garlic is effective to help stop your skin from wrinkling because it contains antioxidants and has the power to restore tissues
- Hard cheeses can prevent cavities and help stop bacteria growth in the mouth
- Yogurt can help with your digestive health, as it contains natural bacteria. Great for fighting tooth decay and helps to keep your teeth whiter
- Vitamins A, C, and potassium (great for skin and hair): Consuming citrus type fruits will help the body form collagen which holds the skin cells together. Be sure to include citrus fruit in your daily diet for its other health benefits like lots of Vitamin C
- Tomatoes which are fruit rather than vegetable are great for the skin and contain quantities of Vitamins A, C and potassium
- Bananas are also a good source of potassium. They contain natural oils and vitamins that help both your skin and your hair

- Sweet potatoes: Excellent for the skin in general. Prevents wrinkles and help the skin been smoother and clearer. Loaded with Vitamin A which does wonders for your skin in general. Your skin will be smoother and clearer

- Green and yellow vegetables and saturated fat to reduce wrinkles [20]

Comprehensive List of Skin Rejuvenation Foods		
Arugula	Dark Chocolate	Papaya
Baby Greens	Extra Virgin Olive Oil	Peaches
Beet Greens	Free Range Organic, Pasture- Raised Chicken	Plums
Berries		Red Bell Pepper
Blue Green Algae	Grass Fed Beef, Lamb, Goat	Red Grapefruit
Broccoli		Red Grapes
Brussel Sprouts	Green, White, Red Rooibos and Oolong Tea	Salmon, Trout, Shrimp, Lobster
Butter (from Grass Fed Cows)		Spinach
Cabbage	Kale	Squash
Cantaloupe	Kiwi	Strawberries
Carrots	Lard	Sweet Potatoes
Cauliflower	Mangoes	Swiss Chard
Cherries	Mustard Greens	Tomatoes
Coconut Oil	Oranges	Watermelon
Cold Water Wild Caught Fish	Organic Coffee	
Collards	Papaya	

Bioactive compounds of anti-ageing foods for young skin	
Bioactive compounds	**Sources**
Resveratrol	Blueberries, cranberries, dark chocolate, pistachios, peanuts, grapes, wine, cocoa
Apigenin	Celery, parsley, oregano, chamomile, artichokes
Silybin	Silymarin
Genistein	Alfalfa, soybean, fava bean, green lentil
Berberine	Barberry, tree turmeric, Oregon grape, goldenseal
Phloretin	Apples, strawberries
Allicin	Garlic
Proanthocyanidins and Anthocyanidins	Fruits and vegetables, such as red cabbage, grapes, and several types of berries (blueberries, strawberries, blackberries, blackcurrants, cranberries, raspberries)

Glowing skin reflects good overall health.

Edua Potor

Beauty and Exercise

Of course, everyone knows that exercising every day is important for weight control but when you exercise you perspire. This clears the body of toxins. As the toxins are released through the pores, they will remain on the skin unless you wash them off after exercising. Failure to do this will increase your chances of getting a fungal or bacterial infection. Here are a few more things to consider:

Exercise also tones the body and skin and the more it is toned the better it will look and feel. The appearance of cellulite can be lessened by toning the muscles. The firmer and stronger the muscles the more elastic the skin will appear

The blood flow and the oxygen level of the body is increased with exercise which in turn flows to the skin. Exercise does relieve stress and advantages of this do extend to your complexion

Exercising helps the skin produce more of its natural oils which will keep your skin looking healthy, glowing, and supple

Reverse Ageing - Face and Body Products

The skin being the largest organ of your body, is naturally designed to release and defend against toxins

Your skin absorbs up to 60% of the ingredients you use daily, including the synthetic and toxic chemicals

It takes only 26 seconds for the chemicals in your personal care products to enter your bloodstream

Most personal care products contain harmful ingredients, synthetic materials and many manufacturers use industrial chemicals which are scientifically proven to be toxic and detrimental to our health

What is contained in the products you are using?

The skincare industry uses very clever marketing messages and produce printed labels with phrases such as "Active/Key ingredients" or "Natural"

The full list of ingredients, often in very small print are fillers that can be harmful to our skin

Deciphering Cosmetic Codes: The main undesirables		
Sulfates "comes from" "derived from" **On Labels:** sodium laureth sulfate (SLES), ammonium laureth sulfate (ALES), sodium lauryl sulfate (SLS) and ammonium lauryl sulfate (ALS)	**Filler:** Contained in 90% products of foaming and lathering fillers – Skin and Hair	Skin irritants, hormone and endocrine disruptors, suspected carcinogens, and gene mutagens Animals exposed to sulfates experience eye damage, central nervous system depression, laboured breathing, diarrhea, and severe skin irritation
Paraben **On Labels:** prefixes ethyl-, methyl-, propyl-, isopropyl-, butyl- or isobutyl	**Preservative**	One of the chemicals foremost responsible for disrupting the endocrine system and unbalancing crucial hormones A 2004 study found paraben in over 90% of human breast cancer tumours
Sodium Benzoate	**Preservative** in skincare, toothpaste, and mouth wash	When mixed with vitamin C and ascorbic acid, sodium benzoate (as well as potassium benzoate) forms benzene, a known carcinogen
Not listed when it is a secondary ingredient of a raw material. For example, "organic Calendula Officinalis Extract" (listed on the label) is sold as a cosmetic raw material with the addition of glycerine and preserved with potassium sorbate and sodium benzoate		
PEG **Polyethylene Glycol**	**Degreaser** used in cosmetics and oven cleaners!	PEG is commonly contaminated with a known carcinogen called 1,4-dioxane – some studies have linked it to leukemia and uterine, breast and brain cancers
Also contains high amounts of heavy metals, and metal contamination, known to cause neurological, autoimmune and kidney issues.		

FD&C Colours and Pigments	Colorants	Classified as either organic or inorganic depending on the chemistry. Organic colours were originally called "coal tar". Inorganic colorants are composed of insoluble metallic compounds
Inorganic colours do not have the same kinds of health risks as organic colours and therefore do not require certification."[i] - When followed by the word **lake**, it means that the pigment is mixed with calcium or aluminium as fixates so the colour stays put on the skin, i.e.: lipstick		
Alcohols **On Labels:** isopropyl alcohol, SD alcohol 40 and ethyl alcohol, ethanol, denatured alcohol, methanol, and benzyl alcohol	**Solvents** made from propylene, a petroleum derivative	A significant amount of research has shown that alcohol may cause free-radical damage to the skin including brown spots, hyperpigmentation, and premature ageing
Urea On Labels: diazolidinyl urea, imidazolidinyl urea and DMDM hydantoin	**Skin exfoliator** and fertilizer: best source of nitrogen	Produced by most plants and animals and found in the top layers of healthy skin. Synthetic urea quickly moves through the natural barrier of the skin and allows the other chemicals in the product to move into the body with it. Primary cause of contact dermatitis
Also contains small amounts of formaldehyde, a carcinogenic chemical that is toxic when inhaled		
Fragrances including Geraniol, Citral and Limonene found in cosmetics are all synthetic	**Perfumes**	Phthalates used to stabilize fragrances are hormone disruptors linked to allergies - may cause headaches, dizziness, allergic rashes, skin discoloration, violent coughing, vomiting and skin irritation

Clinical observation shows fragrances can affect the endocrine and central nervous system, causing depression, hyperactivity, and irritability

Additional negative impacts from: Phthalates, silicones, EDTA, polyethene glycol, formaldehyde-forming compounds, propylene glycol, tap water, mineral oil, methylparaben, Alkyl parahydroxy, Lisoparaben, Propylene alcohol, benzene, paraffin, butyloarabene, Toluene, Petrolatum oxybenzone

- Everything that is applied to the skin is absorbed into the bloodstream, circulates to our cells, and mingles with our mitochondria. We can feed our immune system and skin cells at the same time! Everything that goes in and on your body must benefit your cells and your skin

- Every single ingredient matters and when nature provides such amazing botanicals to attend to our health and beauty, why use anything artificial?

- Skin cells are shed every 35 days and regularly replaced by new cells

- Reprogram your skin cells for health and healing and regeneration

- Skin cells need organic, pure, whole food compounds, essential oils, and the finest nutrients to replicate healthy cells

- Use Natural, botanical ingredients such as aloe vera, essential oils and natural antioxidants

- Use natural and organic ingredients from plant oils and waxes, mineral pigments

- Natural anti-ageing skin care system will support a more youthful appearance!

Natural Ingredients and Anti-ageing Essential Oils		
Bulgarian Rose – Otto Rose	Antiviral – antibacterial	Reduces lines
Turmeric	Anti-allergenic	Stronger antioxidant than vit E
Lavender	Excellent for burns and relaxation	Antiseptic and can reduce scarring
Seabuckthorn	Vitamin C and omega-7	For acne and rosacea, pigmentation, stretch marks, regeneration of tissues
Castor Oil	The queen of skin repair	Cures skin infections, antibacterial, anti-inflammatory. Treats acne, purifies the skin, eliminate rashes, skin blemishes
Basil	Toning of skin	Clarifies acne and skin infections, refreshes
German Chamomille	Healing properties and anti-inflammatory	For acne, burns, cuts, eczema, rashes, insect bites

Rejuvenation with Micro-Needling - Derma roller

Micro needling is a procedure using thin needles to make tiny holes in the top layer of your skin. The damage helps stimulate your skin's healing process so that it produces more collagen and elastin. A handheld device is used for this procedure with a handle at one end and a roller with tiny needles at the other. The size of the needles varies, but the most used is 1 to 1.5 mm.

Micro-needling can be used successfully for a range of skin imperfections, including:

- Acne scars
- Burn scars
- Fine lines and wrinkles

- Stretchmarks
- Hyper-pigmentation
- Dull skin
- Open pores
- Loose, sagging skin

A convincing view of two microscopic photos at 20 times magnification showing before and after images, six weeks after micro-needling proves the formation of new collagen.

Micro-needling creates micro-channels that allows products like serums or peptides to penetrate much more deeply than it usually could when applied topically, so results are revved up. There, they stimulate the body's own stem cells to help repair fine lines and wrinkles and restore the skin's firmness and elasticity.

Rejuvenation with Face-Yoga Exercises

- We have 52 muscles in our face and neck!
- To get younger, naturally, spend 8 minutes each day to exercise those muscles
- Look 10 to 15 years younger in 30 days!
- The 3 most efficient facial exercises are for the eye area, chin, and mid-face

1- Eye Lift Exercise - How To Get Rid of Hooded Eyes

- Spread your fingers
- With forefinger: below your brows, above the eye socket bones, and SLIGHTLY pull upwards and outwards
- With thumb, below your eye socket above the cheekbone
- Hold that pose

164

- Squeeze your eyes shut REALLY TIGHT and count to ten
- Repeat five time until you feel the burn
- Relax

2- How To Firm Up Your Neckline and Get a Sharper Jaw Line

- Open your mouth to form a round letter O
- Roll the lips over the teeth and have them pressing the teeth
- Open and close your mouth 3 times, very slowly
- Whilst opening and closing the mouth, pull the mouth corners upwards like in a big smile
- Whilst opening and closing the mouth, feel the pull of the muscles of the neck and the jaw
- When you completed the first 3 counts, pull the chin up towards the ceiling and repeat
- When completed the second set, pull the chin up a little further and feel the stretch of the neck the jaw and the lips. Feel the burn
- If you can, do a last 3 counts, very slowly
- Relax

3- Firm Up Mid Face Muscle Group, Neck and Chin

1- Allow your mouth to fall slightly open, place forefingers on the hinges of your jaw

- Make small, firm upward circles starting at the jaw hinge
- This exercise will energise the entire face and will strengthen the mid face muscle group

2- Protrude your chin and rhythmically slap the underside of your jawline

- Make sure your hand is stiff as you execute this exercise
- This procedure will open the energy channels along the jawline and elevate sagging skin along the chin and jaw
- The muscles along the jaw will tighten and lift

SUMMARY OF CHAPTER NINE
Ageless Youthful Skin
- Skin ages as we age.
- What causes skin to age?
- Intrinsic vs extrinsic ageing – Inevitable vs controllable
- The connection of the ageing gut and inflammation and ageing skin
- Senolytics – a new class of drugs
  o Quercetin reduces senescence factors in skin
  o Beta Glucans support skin health
  o Zinc protects Gut, skin and immune system
  o Lactobacillus Reuteri and skin rejuvenation
- Foods that improve your appearance from Inside Out
  o For Supple Skin
  o Preventing Wrinkles
  o Comprehensive list for skin rejuvenation
  o Bioactive compounds of anti-ageing foods for young skin
- Beauty and Exercise
- Reverse ageing Face and Body natural products
- What is contained in the products you are using?
- Deciphering Cosmetic Codes: the main undesirable
- Natural ingredients and Anti-ageing Essential Oils
- Rejuvenation with Micro Needling - Derma-Roller
- Rejuvenation with Face -Yoga exercises
  o Eye Lift Exercise - How to get rid of hooded eyes
  o How to firm up your neckline and get a sharper jaw line
  o Firm up mid face muscle group, neck, and chin

CHAPTER TEN

Sleep: Your secret superpower

"It is a common experience that a problem difficult at night is resolved in the morning after the committee of sleep has worked on it."

John Steinbeck

CHAPTER TEN

Sleep: Your secret superpower

Sleep, Your Effective Weapon to Success

We spend a third of our lives sleeping! So many years spent unconscious (or so we think) in bed!

We all want to get the most out of life and sometimes that means sacrificing a few hours of sleep here and there. But are we deluding ourselves by thinking that this will give us more life? Sleep deprivation can lead to physical and mental health issues as well as impairing our ability to think clearly and make decisions. [1]

How Much Should You Sleep? How Much Is Enough? The Sleeping Habits of Highly Successful People

A survey of several CEOs of varying size companies revealed that most executives are aware of the importance of sleep and its impact on productivity and that to take care of your team and your company, you must take care of yourself first.

- Oprah Winfrey reportedly gets 8 hours sleep between 10pm and 6am
- Jeff Bezos said to "The Economist Club" that he needs eight hours of sleep to think better, have more energy and sustain a better mood

- Elon Musk mentioned at the "Joe Rogan Experience" that he needs to ensure getting 6 hours sleep a night

- In her 2010 TED talk "How to succeed? Get more sleep", Arianna Huffington states that achieving eight hours of sleep whilst requiring discipline is the key to a more productive, inspired, and joyful life

- Warren Buffet sleeps 8 hours a night

The American Academy of Sleep Medicine advises that seven hours is the minimum amount of sleep recommended for adults, which is not achieved by more than a third of Americans. Dr. Nathaniel F Watson states that their Consensus Panel found that sleeping six or fewer hours per night is inadequate to sustain health and safety in adults. However, it is also true that the quality of sleep is more important than the quantity of sleep to improve your brain function, longevity and performance in all aspects of life.

Since sleep is right up there with nutrition and exercise in terms of its role in health, make sure to give it the attention it deserves and adjust to your own metabolism and other factors involving your lifestyle routines. If you can't get as many hours as you need at night, it's totally legit to take a nap; just make sure that you do whatever feels right for you.

Sleeping Cycles

It is crucial to understand how our bodies go through four stages during a night's rest and we cycle through each night at about 90 minutes each. [2]

Stages	What Happens – Patterns and Stages [3]	Duration
Stage 1	The brain transitions from waking into sleep. Breathing and heart rate start to slow down, and muscles start to relax. Slow eye movement. Alpha waves begin being replaced by Theta waves – Move from relaxation to light sleep	1 to 5 minutes
Stage 2	Regulatory maintenance of the body takes place - Breathing heart rate regulates – Body temperature drops – Lose sense of place – Slower brain waves - Eye movement stops – Blood pressure drops – Muscles relax – Tissue growth and repair. Alpha waves cease, and Theta waves predominate	25 to 60 minutes
Stage 3 & 4	Deep sleep stage - Physical restorative sleep - Brain waves are at their slowest and longest frequency – Energy is restored – Rejuvenation - hormones are released – Continued slower brain waves – Brain is active dreaming. Delta waves occur	20 to 40 minutes
Stage 5 REM Sleep	REM = Rapid Eye Movement. Mentally restorative sleep - brain moves information from short-term to long-term memory - Muscles are paralysed – Irregular breathing and heart rate – Early awakening	10 to 60 minutes

(Summarised from excerpts out of The Huffington Post - National Sleep Foundation – The Biological Optimization Blueprint)

Dr. Michael Breus, known as "the sleep doctor", explains that we go through four to six sleep cycles per night with an average of 90 minutes each. He further emphasizes that deep sleep is when the body is in a physically restorative state, and it is the "wake up and feel great" sleep.

"You can last three days without water, thirty days without food...you can last seven days without sleep".

Dr. Michael Breus

Chemicals and Hormones Regulating Sleep and Weight Loss

You may find this section of interest as it is the foundation upon which we base our decisions on resolving sleeplessness or improving the quality of our sleep and losing weight!

Adenosine is a chemical that plays an important role in the sleep-awake state. It builds up when we are awake and appears to increase sleep pressure. As it binds to adenosine receptors in the brain, it causes **drowsiness** and blood vessels to dilate to let more oxygen in the brain during sleep. [4]

Caffeine, on the other hand, suppresses adenosine and promotes wakefulness. This is the reason that coffee is not recommended after lunch because it stays in the bloodstream for 10 hours and can mess with your sleep.

Neurotransmitters, the chemical messengers within the nervous system, are involved in promoting wakefulness or sleep and include GABA, acetylcholine, orexin and serotonin. [5] [6]

The most important sleep-related hormones are adrenaline, cortisol, norepinephrine and melatonin, which is the best-known hormone, naturally produced as light exposure decreases. This is why reducing light exposure, especially blue light from computer/phone screens is important an hour before bedtime to prevent impacting on our circadian rhythms and delaying our sleep. [7]

Cortisol levels lower when we enjoy good quality sleep and we become less stressed or anxious and increase our ability to relax. This supports hormone and neurotransmitters balance.

Other significant hormones affected by sleep and circadian disturbance are growth hormones as well as leptin and ghrelin that regulate appetite. [8]

Sleep is one of the most important aspects of our lives, when our body burns fat, builds muscles and repairs our cells.

Furthermore, good quality sleep decreases our cortisol levels, reduces our cravings for food, especially sugars, and increases our growth hormones (cellular rejuvenation) and increases testosterones and progesterone (better sex)!

Research on Sleep Deprivation – Just One Hour!

According to one study by neuroscientists from Harvard Medical School, chronic sleep deprivation can increase the risk of premature death. [9] [10]

Missing just one hour of sleep skyrockets your risk of depression and anxiety. [11]

In this study, Dr. Laura Koniver observed the following findings:

- Each hour of sleep made a statistically significant difference in the rates of depression, hopelessness, nervousness, restlessness and fidgeting
- Just one more hour of sleep significantly alleviated every single one of these symptoms
- One less hour of sleep increased the rate of symptoms by 60 to 80%!

- 6 hours of sleep instead of 7 raised the rate of nervousness (by 80%) and depression (by 77%)

- These rates compounded with each additional hour!

- Getting two hours less sleep TRIPLED the rates of nervousness and hopelessness and almost QUADRUPLED the rates of depression and restlessness

Burnout and Sleep-Deprived Executives

Burnout is a common work-related occupational syndrome amongst executives who must perform and keep performing in demanding, high-pressure and sometimes chaotic environments. They mostly have very high job expectations and in times of economic challenges possibly a sense of having little control over their work. Executives, specifically CEOs, are always expected to deliver without much recognition for their efforts.

> **"There is a time for many words, and there is also a time for sleep."**
>
> Homer

High achiever personalities are competitive, driven and have high expectation of themselves and their employees. They often take on too many responsibilities and find it hard to allocate time for socializing or relaxing. They may not block time for exercise which would affect their sleep and further impact their burnout state. [12] [13]

There is a considerable connection between sleep and burnout, so improving sleep may prevent burnout. [14]

It is important to be aware of your mental state and recognize that burnout has occurred. At this stage, self-reflection is useful to identify what led to the situation and to address the issue that created it. [15][16]

Looking After Yourself Is Essential

Look after your basic needs: take a break from work to reset.

Ensure that you get sufficient quality sleep to restore your batteries and aim for 8 hours per night and implement good sleeping habits. [17][18]

The Burnout Fix, from Dr. Jacinta M. Jiménez, Stanford-trained psychologist, former Global Head of Coaching at "BetterUp", and coach to Silicon Valley's top performers, reveals how to harness science-backed resilience strategies to buffer against burnout and thrive in today's workforce. [19]

She suggests that we are subject to additional new challenges with the increasing growth of new technology applications and that most companies are "pushing through, regardless". Whilst science stipulates that resiliency can be beneficial, the consequences of overwork are more complex and that continuously living on the edge carries the danger of losing our humanity and our vitality.

In her book "The Burnout Fix", Dr. Jacinta M. Jiménez suggest some researched solutions such as:

- Recognize burn-out and respond quickly
- Question the fairness of work such as workload
- Check if your values are still aligned
- Acknowledge your needs for reward/recognition
- Resilience to recharge yourself, take care of yourself so that you can take care of what you need to impact on the world

Some sleeping Tips and Hacks [20] [21]

- Regularity – go to bed at the same time and get up at the same time
- Optimize your sleep with light:
  - Eliminate the blue light before bed – any screen light
  - Last hour before bed, dim your lights in your home
  - Sleep in total darkness
  - Expose your eyes with blue light or natural sunlight in the morning (To quick start your circadian rhythm)
- Temperature – keep cool – About 18 degrees. (Core temperature 1 degree cooler than your body)
- If you suffer from insomnia – get up and do something different/meditate
- Good mattress to eliminate pressure points
- No coffee after lunch
- Alcohol can interfere with your REM sleep – if you must – have one glass of red
- Meal timing – no food at least 4 hours before bedtime
- Shift your brain before bed:
  - Meditate at least 5 mins before bed
  - Write a gratitude list and feel it in your heart
  - Brain dumps – put your thoughts on paper to quieten your mind
- No sugars as it raises cortisol and lowers GABA and serotonin
- Exercise especially muscle-building workouts preferably earlier in the day or light exercise like walking at the latest 2 hours before bedtime
- Sleep and weight loss; the 2 appetite hormones are Leptin (sated) and Grelin (hungry)

o If sleep is limited to 6 hours for example: Leptin decreases by 18% and Grelin, the hungry hormone, increases by 28% resulting in increased eating of 300 to 400 calories, especially heavy carbs, simple sugars, and high sodium as well as increasing your BP!!

- Sleeping and dreaming

  o Whilst dreaming and during REM stage, the brain moves into problem solving
  o Dreaming has the capacity to detox an emotional memory like an overnight therapy

Some of the Best Sleep Supplements

- Magnesium

- L-Theanine (100-400mg before bed)

- Lavender Oil

- Ashwagandha

- Reishi

- CBD

- 5-HTP, precursor to melatonin

- Melatonin; 3mg scientifically proven dose of the sleep hormone shown to best aid deep sleep

- GABA boosting supplements: Passionflower, chamomile, lemon balm, and theanine all induce a state of relaxation that helps us calm down by increasing GABA signalling

- Glycine: with GABA, most important inhibitor neurotransmitter, promoting a calm mind and improves sleep quality

www.TheAgelessExecutive.com

- D-ribose to support mitochondrial energy production and increase sleep quality

- Zeaxanthin (cross the blood brain barrier and helps with brain recovery)

- Perfect Aminos

Sleeping Habits of the Highly Successful: [22]

- Oprah Winfrey: her last and first thoughts of the day is centred upon gratitude." The last thing I do before I go to sleep is to write five things that gave me great pleasure or that I was grateful for"

- Jeff Bezos - founder of Amazon - spends "pottering time" in the mornings which sets the tone for his ability to relax at night, knowing he will have time for himself in the morning before starting his first meeting at 10am

- Jack Ma – co-founder of Alibaba advises: "Sleep well, no matter what. Problems will always be there, but if I sleep well, I have a better chance to fight against them"

- Elon Musk – Tesla and SpaceX – "If I sleep less than 6 hours, total productivity decreases"

- Arianna Huffington, media mogul :"To succeed, get more sleep! Turn off all devices and read a (physical) book before bed

- Tobi Lutke – founder of Shopify:" Get plenty of time for sleep and rest. My job is incredible, but it's also just a job. Family and personal health rank higher in my priority list"

- Warren Buffet, investor, values his sleep and is in bed by 10.45pm to enjoy a full eight hours of sleep

- Bill Gates, Microsoft Co-Founder gives the following tips: "Replace LED bulbs in your bedroom, with incandescent bulbs which emit a warm and soft light that is less likely to disrupt your circadian rhythm or melatonin production, limit alcohol intake, consider taking a midday nap and ensure a temperature of around 18°C"

Natural Sleep Supports

There is nothing better than a cup of tea to relax and unwind before bed. Tea has been used for centuries to soothe the mind and body, and it can be enjoyed in many ways. Obviously, when you are looking for a bedtime tea to help you sleep, stick with herbal options favouring a few blends of herbs and roots.

Hops	Hops are the flowers of the Humulus Lupulus, often used to flavour beer but can also be brewed into tea. Hops have sedative effects and can help promote sleep
Chamomile	Chamomile is a flower often dried and brewed into tea. Chamomile used as a natural remedy for centuries, helps with anxiety and insomnia. Chamomile tea may work by increasing glycine levels which has calming and relaxing effects on the nervous system
Lavender	This beautiful purple flower plant is often used in teas and aromatherapy to promote relaxation. One study found that lavender tea helped people sleep better and feel refreshed the following day
Valerian	Valerian is a flowering plant used as an herbal remedy to treat anxiety and insomnia. Valerian root has been shown to increase levels of gamma-aminobutyric acid (GABA) in the brain, a neurotransmitter with calming and relaxing effects
Lemon Balm	Lemon balm is a perennial herbaceous plant in the mint family and may work by increasing levels of GABA in the brain
Passionflower	A vine with white, purple, or blue flowers. Studies suggest that purple passionflower extract can help manage sleep irregularities and relieve anxiety
Skullcap	Skullcap is a flowering plant belonging to the mint family and commonly used as a sedative in blends with other herbs like valerian

Amazingly Simple Breathing Exercise Before Going to Bed

This breathing exercise is designed to help you sleep better by switching on the PNS. (Parasympathetic Nervous System).

Breathwork has experienced a modern resurgence and there are at least 50 offshoots of breathwork been practised around the world.

The art of moving the breath through the body to create a feeling of bliss, involves breathing that controls the breath.

The simplification of what happens when you breathe is that when you breathe in, you inhale oxygen and when you breathe out, you exhale carbon dioxide (CO_2).

CO_2 relaxes the muscles surrounding your airways, arteries and capillaries, helping to increase blood flow to different parts of the body like the brain, heart and muscles.

During nasal breathing, nitric oxide is released into the nasal airways, traveling with inspiration to the lower airways and the lungs where it increases the oxygen uptake in the blood. Through the dilation of air passages and blood vessels, nitric oxide plays a critical role in blood circulation functioning along with communication between brain cells. [23]

This is why nasal breathing is encouraged, furthermore, it can significantly enhance your sexual prowess!

This is one of the 9 breathing techniques, a simplified form of Pranayama, the most beneficial according to scientific research.

You will fall asleep much easier and feel refreshed and rejuvenated in the morning.

How to do it:

- Step 1: Sit comfortably with your back straight
- Step 2: Inhale deeply through your nose (or mouth)
- Step 3: Gently and slowly breathe out of your mouth as though breathing through a straw
- Step 4: As you exhale, imagine a wave of relaxation flowing down your body from the top of your head to the soles of your feet and the tips of your toes
- Step 5: Once you have exhaled, hold your breath for a few seconds before inhaling and inhaling deeply
- Step 6: Repeat the process for 5-10 minutes

Just start with 5 minutes to experience the benefits of a restful, deep, refreshing sleep.

Music for Sleep and Rediscovering The Solfeggio Scale [24]

Every sound ... every wave, signal and motion create a frequency. Frequencies are measured with a unit called hertz (Hz). It's simply the rate at which a frequency vibrates.

A musical frequency is another form of vibration. There are 9 (nine) frequencies in the Solfeggio scale, and they are mathematically consistent with the patterns of our universe.

The most popular ancient 6-tone scale caries the ability to influence and transform wellbeing, and in this instance, to support your relaxation and sleep.

Brain Waves	Qualities	Frequencies	Solfeggio scale	Qualities
Gamma	Maintain focus while awake	30 to 50 Hz	396 Hz	Liberation from Fear
Beta	Promotes concentration and focus	13 to 30 Hz	417 Hz	Facilitating Change
Alpha	Awake and relaxed	7 to 13 Hz	528 Hz	Transformation and Love
Theta	Meditation, creativity, "in the zone"	4 to 7 Hz	639 Hz	Connecting and Relationships
Delta	Deep, dreamless sleep	0.5 to 4 Hz	741 Hz	Expression and Solutions

According to Professor Willi Apel, a German American musicologist, you access theta and delta brain waves with the ancient tones of Solfeggio frequencies, allowing you to experience deep relaxation and improved sleep quality. These frequencies have been used for centuries to promote healing, balance and spiritual growth. By listening to these tones you can access theta and delta brain waves which are associated with deep relaxation and improved sleep quality. This can further help reduce stress levels, improve concentration and increase overall wellbeing. These frequencies can also be used to create a calming atmosphere in your home or office environment. With regular use of Solfeggio frequencies, you can experience improved sleep quality as well as enhanced mental clarity and focus.

As reported in the documentation provided in "Healing Codes for the Biological Apocalypse", Dr. Joseph Puleo was introduced to the Pythagorean method of numeral reduction. [25] He suggests that our modern-day musical scale is out of sync when compared with the original Solfeggio scale.

If we want to bring harmony in our lives, we need to replace the dissonant western scale with the Solfeggio scale and let the music become once again a tool to raise human nature and a method to connect us with the source of spirit and divinity.

Nikola Tesla said, "If you only knew the magnificence of the 3, 6 and 9, then you would hold a key to the universe." The 3, 6, and 9 are the fundamental root vibrations of the Solfeggio frequencies.

Albert Einstein stated: "Concerning matter, we have been all wrong. What we have called matter is energy, whose vibration has been so lowered as to not be perceptible to the senses. There is no matter."

As recognized by science, all matter beings vibrate at specific rates, and everything has its own melody, from atoms to galaxies.

That is why these Solfeggio frequencies are so powerful. They can literally bring you back to the original tones of the galaxies and put your body into a balanced resonance.

You will find many musical tracks on YouTube at the right "sleep vibration" level to soothe your brain, calm your mind and support your sleep.

SUMMARY OF CHAPTER TEN

Sleep: Your Secret Superpower

- Sleep, your effective weapon to success
- How much should you sleep? How much is enough?
- How much do highly successful people sleep?
- Sleeping Cycles
- Chemicals and Hormones regulating sleep and weight loss
- Research on sleep deprivation – Just one hour!
- Burnout and sleep deprived Executives
- Looking after yourself is essential
- Some sleeping tips and hacks
- Some of the best sleep supplements
- Sleeping habits of the highly successful
- Natural Sleep Supports
- Amazingly simply breathing exercise before going to bed
- Music for sleep and rediscovering the Solfeggio scale

CONGRATULATIONS

Congratulations on completing the reading of "The Ageless Executive" and welcome to this pivotal conclusion, completing the transformative journey of this book, unlocking the secrets of peak performance for ageless executives. In the previous ten chapters we have explored a wealth of scientifically based information, insights, strategies and practical wisdom designed specifically to empower driven professionals like you to optimize your health, well-being and overall performance. As a high-achieving executive, you understand the demands of your dynamic role and the critical need to maintain a competitive edge while navigating a fast-paced, ever-evolving business landscape.

This book contains the core principles and offers key takeaways for achieving and sustaining peak performance for you, the ageless executive. Prepare to delve into the essential strategies that will enable you to thrive, balancing your professional ambitions with your physical vitality, mental clarity and emotional resilience. As you apply the information and principles of this book, get ready to embark on a transformative journey towards unlocking your full potential. Embrace these teachings, make conscious choices, and thrive on your journey to optimal well-being.

ABOUT THE AUTHOR

International Author - Presenter - Researcher - Executive Coach

Edua Potor is a Global Executive Search Researcher, experienced in identifying C Level Executives and Boards. She searched for and interviewed well over 15,000 executive candidates.

During those interviews, Edua acquired a good understanding of the stresses and health risks faced by Senior Executives. Combining her own personal experience in recovery and her thorough study and research in the fields of health and longevity, Edua reveals in her new book, THE AGELESS EXECUTIVE, critical breakthrough strategies to upgrade your body, melt away excess weight, get younger and rejuvenate your brain!

She studied, researched, trained with and learned from, experts and leaders in health, wellness and mind management and accumulated a wealth of information from scientists all around the world, some of which were awarded Nobel prizes for their discoveries of the keys to ageing, life span and health span.

Edua started her life in East Europe, where her family experienced the Hungarian uprising against communism, fleeing to Austria as political refugees. They experienced further expulsions from countries undergoing political turmoil, mainly in the Congo, Ruanda, and Burundi. She then made an easy choice to relocate to Australia!

She lived in and visited 23 countries, was drawn to spiritual studies, eastern philosophies, and healing modalities, and learned 5 languages. English is her fifth language, and she is still fluent in French.

She has a bachelor's degree in Homeopathic Medicine (BHM), AdvDip PR and a Graduate Certificate in English Language and Literature from the University of Oxford.

She is an enthusiastic student of life, health, consciousness, and longevity, aspiring to the marriage of health, science, spirit, and business.

Edua has established herself on the beautiful Sunshine Coast of Queensland, Australia and starts each day walking barefoot on the beach or trekking through sand dunes and forests.

Her mission is to revolutionise wellness, its perception and importance, in the workplace.

The Ageless Executive – Home Study MASTERCLASS

"The Ultimate Course About Becoming an Ageless Executive: Mastering Peak Performance and Longevity – In the boardroom, workplace, and life."

Are you ready to unlock the secrets to becoming an Ageless Executive? In today's fast-paced world, where health is paramount for success, this masterclass is designed to empower you with the knowledge and tools to achieve peak performance and longevity.

Discover the critical steps necessary to transform not only your own health but also the health of your employees. Learn how to implement a permanent shift in your well-being, resulting in superior performance that transcends the boardroom and positively impacts all aspects of your life.

Failure to have a comprehensive health plan can be detrimental to both personal and professional success. This masterclass will enlighten you on the risks of neglecting your health and provide you with the essential information and breakthroughs to navigate the next 5 to 10 years with confidence.

Through self-paced study, you will digest critical information at your own convenience. More importantly, you will learn how to implement essential steps for permanent health vibrancy and brain rejuvenation. We believe that true success lies in aligning personal and professional well-being, and this masterclass will guide you towards achieving just that.

Our comprehensive program includes a list of proven strategies to upgrade your body, shed excess weight, and rejuvenate your brain. You'll uncover the secrets to avoiding burnout, overcoming adrenal addiction, and regulating cortisol levels, allowing you to experience extraordinary health and vitality in all areas of your life.

Each module of this masterclass comes with a dedicated workbook, providing you with a tangible tool to track your progress and ensure your success along the way. Our expert educator, Edua Potor, combines ancient wisdom with cutting-edge scientific knowledge to deliver an ongoing peak performance experience like no other.

To embark on this exceptional journey and find out more about The Ageless Executive Masterclass, visit our website today. Take the first step toward becoming an Ageless Executive, ready to conquer the challenges of the modern world while achieving optimal health, vitality, and success.

The Ageless Executive Intensive Retreat:

Unleashing Peak Performance and Longevity Mastery

Welcome to the exclusive and transformative experience of The Ageless Executive Intensive, led by executive coach Edua Potor. This private 3-day coaching and elite mastermind training workshop/ retreat is designed to propel you to new heights of success in health, performance, and longevity.

Drawing from the most effective research, health strategies and global scientific discoveries, Edua Potor will share their unparalleled expertise, experience and knowledge, exclusively with a select group of individuals. This intensive workshop will take place in a luscious and opulent resort setting, providing the perfect backdrop for your personal transformation.

Prepare to be immersed in information-packed days that are filled with practical data and empowering experiences. **The Ageless Executive Intensive** is a team effort, bringing together professionals who can help you elevate your personal, professional, and health success.

Throughout this intensive program, Edua will personally guide you in creating a new health plan, forging a new path and adopting new patterns for your future health and peak performance. You will discover how to create your own health blueprint to upgrade your body, unlocking the essential elements that will lead to becoming a health-savvy executive.

Topics covered during the workshop include:

- Unleashing Your Potential: Edua will bridge the gap between where you are now and where you want to be, empowering you to tap into your untapped health potential

- Embracing the Mindset of Health-Savvy CEOs: Learn the attitudes, practices and habits of successful CEOs who prioritize their health, and how you can emulate their success

- Building a Health Brand: Discover the essential elements required to build a strong health brand, both for yourself and for your organization

- Instant Credibility and Employee Engagement: Learn how to create instant credibility with your employees when it comes to their health and inspire them to embark on their own wellbeing journeys

- Modelling Health Excellence: Gain insights into modelling health excellence and creating a positive ripple effect throughout your organization

- Networking and Collaboration: Connect with like-minded health executives, share valuable tips for improving company health, and foster collaborative relationships

- Have fun with some unexpected surprises!

And much more...

This exclusive mastermind workshop is reserved for a select number of individuals who are truly committed to their health and ready to embrace the rewards that await them. The question is, will you seize this opportunity and become one of the fortunate few to experience **The Ageless Executive Intensive**?

Join us for this life-changing event and embark on a journey towards peak performance, longevity mastery, and unparalleled success in every area of your life. The path to becoming an Ageless Executive starts here.

The Ageless Executive's Mission

The Ageless Executive upholds the conviction that caring for one another and safeguarding our planet is an inherent trait of humanity. This belief aligns with the contemporary CEO's vision of being a human-centered, responsible and conscientious global leader who not only delivers sustainable value to shareholders but also prioritizes the development of exceptional talent and strives to create a better world.

We extend a warm invitation to you, whether as an individual or a company, to actively embrace and support this belief by contributing to the causes and initiatives championed by remarkable entities.

If you are open to suggestions, here are some of our favourites:

• **Charity Water**

https://www.charitywater.org/about

The charity's goal is to end the global water crisis.

- **Water.Org**

https://water.org/about-us/

A global nonprofit to bring water and sanitation to the world.

- **The ocean cleanup**

https://theoceancleanup.com/

A non-profit to remove 90% of floating plastic pollution & restore the health of our oceans.

- **Kiva**

https://www.kiva.org/about

It's a loan, not a donation. A global nonprofit to enhance financial inclusion and to provide loans, unlocking capital for those in need.

- **The Fred Hollows Foundation.**

https://www.hollows.org/au/about-the-foundation

To eliminate avoidable blindness and improving Indigenous Australian health and to restore sight.

- **White Lion.**

https://www.whitelion.asn.au/

An Australian social enterprise dedicated to preventing young people in the justice system from reoffending aiming to enhance their reintegration into society and to transform their lives.

With deep gratitude

REFERENCES – NOTES – BIBLIOGRAPHY

As an author and avid pursuer of knowledge, I am pleased to present this compilation of notes and references that accompany the pages of this book. In assembling this index, I must preface the following annotations with the knowledge that they do not strictly adhere to any specific academic conventions. Instead, they are fashioned in a manner that, while not conforming to established rules, ensures utmost clarity in attributing the sources of the information presented.

Throughout the writing process, my primary aim has been to present a seamless flow of knowledge, free from the constraints of formal citation styles. My intention is to provide readers with a comprehensive record of the sources that have influenced the content within this work while maintaining readability and accessibility.

The decision to eschew academic rigidity in favour of a more reader-friendly approach stems from the belief that knowledge should be easily digestible and readily accessible to all curious minds. In this pursuit, the simplicity of this annotation format is aimed to facilitate your journey into deeper realms of exploration should you wish to embark upon it.

Each entry within this index serves as a gateway to further information, enabling you to delve into the roots of the concepts and ideas presented herein. I encourage you to explore these references, embark on your own intellectual expeditions and broaden your understanding beyond the confines of this volume.

In closing, I extend my heartfelt gratitude to all readers who embark on this intellectual voyage with me. Your quest for knowledge is a testament to the boundless human curiosity that has driven the advancement of our collective understanding throughout history.

Wishing you a profound and enlightening journey.

Chapter 1 - Hydration

(1   Batmanghelidj, Fereydoon, *Your Body's Many Cries for Water* (1992), Global Health Solutions.
ISBN 0- 9629942-3-5

(2)   https://www.washingtonpost.com/wp-dyn/articles/A64133-2004Nov19.html
Physician Fereydoon Batmanghelidj; Wrote About Water's Healing. (n.d.). Retrieved 9 25, 2022

(3)   https://www.usgs.gov/special-topics/water-science-school/science/alkalinity-and-water
Alkalinity and Water I U.S. Geological Survey

(4)   https://theberkey.com/blogs/water-filter/alkalinity-of-water-definition-what-is-the-alkalinity-in-drinking-water
Alkalinity Of Water Definition: What Is the Alkalinity In Drinking Water?

(5)   www.avogel.co.uk/health/circulation/how-does-water-help-circulation/
What role does water play in the circulatory system?

(6)   https://www.alkaway.com.au/education-article/water-alkalinity-and-ph-explained/
Water Alkalinity and pH explained

(7)   https://www.flaska.eu/water-structuring/pioneers-of-water-research/viktor-　schauberger

(8)   https://www.alivewater.ca/viktor-schauberger/

The Water Wizard: The Extraordinary Properties of Natural Water: Paperback 5 Nov1999 - by Viktor Schauberger (Author) – Gateway publishers

He observed that modern man, without realizing it, was destroying the earth, and sabotaging his own cultures by working against Nature. Unfortunately, not much has changed, and his vision of how humanity must work so-operatively with nature if we are to have a future, is perhaps more relevant than ever.

Schauberger had a clear vision of how fertility could be restored to the earth. As an inventor he developed a few ingenious machines which would revolutionize farming, horticulture, forestry and aircraft propulsion. He also developed water purification systems and showed how air and water could be harnessed as fuels for many machines.

(9)   https://hydrationfoundation.org/hydrate-now-course/
Hydration Foundation

(10)   https://www.youtube.com/watch?v=twR5fdnQSkE
Hydration On A Cellular Level (Micro Clustering)

(11)   Dr. Gerald H. Pollack/ is a scientist recognized worldwide as a dynamic speaker and author, whose passion lies in plumbing the depths of natural truths. He received the 1st *Emoto Peace Prize* and is a recipient of the University of Washington's highest honour,

the Annual Faculty Lecturer Award. He is founding Editor-in-Chief of the research journal WATER and Director of the Institute for Venture Science. Dr. Pollack's (award-winning) books include: *The Fourth Phase of Water* (2013), and *Cells, Gels, and the Engines of Life* (2001).

(12)   https://thewellnessenterprise.com/dr-gerald-pollack/
        Three Reasons Why You Need to Know the Name Dr. Gerald Pollack

(13)   https://www.youtube.com/watch?v=FpbuVzXSkos
        Ep 39 Part 1 - Dr. Gerald Pollack "Science of Water"

        Dr. Gerald Pollack maintains an active laboratory at the University of Washington in Seattle. He is the Founding Editor-in-Chief of WATER: A Multidisciplinary Research Journal; Executive

        Director of the Institute for Venture Science; co-founder of 4th-Phase Inc.; and founder of the Annual Conference on the Physics, Chemistry, and Biology of Water.

(14)   https://www.scribd.com/podcast/594071929/Encore-The-Science-of-Water-Gerald-H-Pollack-PhD-Professor-of-Bioengineering-at-the-University-of-Washington-speaks-with-host-Sharon-Kleyne-about

        Gerald H. Pollack, PhD -Professor of Bioengineering at the University of Washington, speaks. with host Sharon Kleyne about the topic of science and water.

        RELEASED: Jun 6, 2022 – Format - Podcast Episode

(15)   Fourth Phase of Water: Beyond Solid, Liquid, and Vapor
        Paperback – 1 May 2013
        Publisher : Ebner and Sons Publishers
        ISBN-10 – 0962689548
        ISBN-13 - 978-0962689543
        by Gerald Pollack (Author), Ethan Pollack (Illustrator)
        Dr. Gerald H Pollack, Dr. Mae Wan Ho, John Stuart Reid and MJ Pangman, 4 scientists who explored the many broad applications of the discovery of the "Fourth Phase" of water and how it will revolutionize all fields of science.

(16)   PubMed Central – International Journal of Molecular Sciences
        Int J Mol Sci. 2020 Jul; 21(14): 5041.
        Published online 2020 Jul 17. doi: 10.3390/ijms21145041
        PMCID: PMC7404113
        PMID: 32708867
        Exclusion Zone Phenomena in Water—A Critical Review of Experimental Findings and Theories
        Daniel C. Elton,1,* Peter D. Spencer,2,* James D. Riches,3 and Elizabeth D. Williams4

(17)   Sharma A., Adams C., Cashdollar B.D., Li Z., Nguyen N.V., Sai H., Shi J., Velchuru G., Zhu K.Z.,
        Pollack G.H. Effect of Health-Promoting Agents on Exclusion-Zone Size. *Dose-Response.* 2018;16:155932581879693. doi: 10.1177/1559325818796937.

(18)   Pokorný J., Pokorný J., Foletti A., Kobilková J., Vrba J., Vrba J. Mitochondrial Dysfunction and Disturbed Coherence: Gate to Cancer. *Pharmaceuticals.* 2015;8:675–695. doi: 10.3390/ph8040675.

(19)   Hwang S.G., Lee H.S., Lee B.C., Bahng G. Effect of Antioxidant Water on the Bioactivities of

Cells. *Int. J. Cell Biol.* 2017;2017:1–12. doi: 10.1155/2017/1917239.

(20)   Tychinsky V.P. Extension of the concept of an anomalous water component to images of T-cell organelles. *J. Biomed. Opt.* 2014;19:126008. doi: 10.1117/1.JBO.19.12.126008.

(21)   How to increase energy in your body with Structured (EZ) Water

https://www.youtube.com/watch?v=y-qgeFXvs_4

Learn how to increase energy in your cells with structure (EZ)water in this interview with Dr. Gerald Pollack, world-renowned Scientist and biomedical engineer. Dr. Gerald Pollack explains the fourth phase of water, Structured (EZ) water. Structured water is a profound scientific discovery and provides us with a deeper understanding of how essential this is to our cells. Awareness of the 4th state of water broadened the new perspectives of how water works in our body and the critical roles of Structured water in our body. Dr. Pollack introduced us to 6 ways to increase EZ water in our body, simple things we can do to charge up our human cells. We invite you to start applying these 6 simple steps to achieve well-being.

Other related links:

Links: Pollack Laboratory: https://www.pollacklab.org/

Water Bridge: https://www.youtube.com/watch?v=iC8KDYcdiUl

Article about the Discovery: http://www.i-sis.org.uk/liquidCrystallineWater.php

TEDx Talk: https://www.youtube.com/watch?v=i-T7tCMUDXU

(22)   https://daveasprey.com/ez-water/#:~:text=EZ%20water%20is%20a%20special,you%20can%20produce%20more%20energy.

(23)   17Vegetables Highest in Water

Written by Daisy Whitbread, BSc (Hons) MSc DipIONPowered by USDA Nutrition Data

Last Updated: April 24th, 2022

https://www.myfooddata.com/articles/vegetables-high-in-water.php

(24)   https://hydrationfoundation.org/hydrate-now-course/

The Hydration Foundation

(25)   Resting Potential ! Definition, Biology and Action Potential

https://www.britannica.com/science/resting-potential

The resting potential of electrically excitable cells lies in the range of **−60 to −95 millivolts** (1 millivolt = 0.001 volt), with the inside of the cell negatively charged

Individual cancer cells have a more positive resting membrane potential than other somatic cell types, in the range of **−30 to −20 mV**, making them more similar to proliferative cell types such as embryonic and stem cells than healthy differentiated cells.

(26)   Where is the water of Kane?7 Yonder on mountain peak, On the ridges steep, In the valleys deep, Where the rivers sweep; There is the water of Kane. From Unwritten Literature of Hawaii: The Sacred Songs of the Hula, translated by N. S. Emerson (Washington, D.C. Smithsonian Institution, Bureau of American Ethnology, Government Printing Office. 1909).

(27)   https://en.wikipedia.org/wiki/Masaru_Emoto (Who is Masaru Emoto?)

(28)   http://spirituality-health.com/articles/latest-message-water-dr-emoto-spiritual-madoff

Kiesling, S. (n.d.). **Latest message from water**: Is Dr. Emoto a spiritual Madoff? Retrieved 9 25, 2022, from

(29)   https://masaru-emoto.net/en/crystal/Masaru Emoto – Photo Gallery of crystals

(30)   Dr. Leonard G. Horowitz is an internationally known authority in the overlapping fields of

public health, behavioural science, emerging diseases, and natural healing.

A Harvard University trained expert in health education and media persuasion, he has additional expertise in genetics and electrogenetics, virology, and vaccine research and development, by reason of his academic trainings, scientific publications, <u>sixteen published books</u>, and internationally recognized authority in these fields.

(31)   DNA: Pirates Of The Sacred Spiral

by Leonard G. Horowitz

ASIN: 0923550453

(32)   <u>http://phoenixaquua.blogspot.com/2010/05/history-of-solfeggio-frequencies.html</u>

(33)   <u>DNA Repair – love meditation</u>

(34)   <u>http://www.youtube.com/watch?v=CQUGUDc-fZQ&feature=related</u>

(35)   <u>http://phoenixaquua.blogspot.com/2009/07/dr-leonard-horowitz.html</u>

(36)   Quench: Beat Fatigue, Drop Weight, and Heal Your Body Through the New Science of Optimum Hydration

Dana Cohen MD and Gina Bria

Hachette Books – New York- Boston

Chapter Two - Nutrition

(1)   sources: American-Heart.org – NYTimes.com – termlifeinsurance.org

(2)   <u>https://pubmed.ncbi.nlm.nih.gov/26866783/</u>

Development of the Yale Food Addiction Scale Version 2.0

Ashley N Gearhardt et al.

(3)   <u>https://link.springer.com/chapter/10.1007/978-1-4757-9071-9_16</u>

DNA Damage by Mercury Compounds: An Overview

Max Costa et al.

(4)   <u>https://www.ewg.org/</u>

EGM's Dirty Dozen and Clean Fifteen Lists

(5)   <u>www.giveproject.org</u>

The Give Project

(6)   <u>https://www.weightwatchers.com/us/blog/food/high-protein-foods</u>

<u>https://facty.com/lifestyle/wellness/ten-of-the-best-high-protein-foods/15/</u>

Links and References

<u>https://www.healthline.com/nutrition/29-cheap-healthy-foods</u>

<u>https://www.healthline.com/nutrition/12-best-foods-to-eat-in-morning</u>

<u>https://www.healthline.com/nutrition/10-super-healthy-high-fat-foods</u>

<u>https://www.healthline.com/nutrition/44-healthy-low-carb-foods</u>

<u>https://www.healthline.com/nutrition/11-most-nutrient-dense-foods-on-the-planet</u>

<u>https://www.healthline.com/nutrition/healthy-eating-for-beginners#section10</u>

https://www.healthline.com/nutrition/purified-vs-distilled-vs-regular-water
https://www.healthline.com/health/healthy-holiday
https://www.healthline.com/nutrition/microgreens
https://www.healthline.com/health/favorite-healthy-finds-raw-vegan-live-love-fruit
https://www.healthline.com/nutrition/top-10-nutrition-facts
https://www.healthline.com/nutrition
https://www.healthline.com/nutrition/reishi-mushroom-benefits
https://www.healthline.com/nutrition/asparagus-benefits
https://www.healthline.com/nutrition/collagen-benefits
https://www.healthline.com/nutrition/sea-cucumber
https://www.healthline.com/nutrition/foods-for-hair-growth
https://www.healthline.com/nutrition/methionine
https://www.healthline.com/nutrition/castor-oil

https://pubmed.ncbi.nlm.nih.gov/14522753/

    Sugars and dental caries

    Riva Touger-Decker, et al.

https://www.ars.usda.gov/northeast-area/beltsville-md-bhnrc/beltsville-human-nutrition-research-center/food-surveys-research-group/docs/fndds-download-databases/

    Food and Nutrient Database for Dietary Studies

    FNDDS At A Glance Factsheet

    Foods and Beverages.xlsx
    Portions and Weights.xlsx
    FNDDS Ingredients.xlsx
    Ingredient Nutrient Values.xlsx
    FNDDS Nutrient Values.xlsx

https://fdc.nal.usda.gov/fdc-app.html#/food-details/170108/nutrients

    FoodData Central.

    Food Category:Vegetables and Vegetable Products

https://pubmed.ncbi.nlm.nih.gov/12730414/

    Concentrations of choline-containing compounds and betaine in common foods

    Steven H Zeisel et al.

https://www.healthline.com/nutrition/21-reasons-to-eat-real-food#TOC_TITLE_HDR_2

https://www.ahajournals.org/doi/full/10.1161/01.cir.0000052939.59093.45

    Markers of Inflammation and Cardiovascular Disease

    Thomas A. Pearson et al.

https://pubmed.ncbi.nlm.nih.gov/27502053/

    Wholesome Nutrition: an example for a sustainable diet

    Karl von Koerber et al.

https://www.cell.com/cell-host-microbe/fulltext/S1931-3128(17)30497-3?_returnURL=https%3A%2F%2Flinkinghub.elsevier.com%2Fretrieve%2Fpii%2FS1931312817304973%3Fshowall%3Dtrue

Fiber-Mediated Nourishment of Gut Microbiota Protects against Diet-Induced Obesity by Restoring IL-22-Mediated Colonic Health

Jun Zou et al

https://pubmed.ncbi.nlm.nih.gov/21676152/

Effects of dietary fibre on subjective appetite, energy intake and body weight: a systematic review of randomized controlled trials

A J Wanders et al.

https://pubmed.ncbi.nlm.nih.gov/17583796/

A Palaeolithic diet improves glucose tolerance more than a Mediterranean-like diet in individuals with ischaemic heart disease

S Lindeberg et al.

https://pubmed.ncbi.nlm.nih.gov/19735513/

Eating chocolate can significantly protect the skin from UV light

Stefanie Williams et al.

https://pubmed.ncbi.nlm.nih.gov/20978772/

Polyhydroxylated fatty alcohols derived from avocado suppress inflammatory response and provide non-sunscreen protection against UV-induced damage in skin cells

Gennady Rosenblat et al.

https://pubmed.ncbi.nlm.nih.gov/11293471/

Skin wrinkling: can food make a difference?

M B Purba et al.

https://pubmed.ncbi.nlm.nih.gov/20085665/

Association of dietary fat, vegetables and antioxidant micronutrients with skin ageing in Japanese women

Chisato Nagata et al.

https://bmjopen.bmj.com/content/3/12/e004277

Do healthier foods and diet patterns cost more than less healthy options? A systematic review and meta-analysis

Mayuree Rao et al

https://pubmed.ncbi.nlm.nih.gov/23468086/

Economic costs of diabetes in the U.S. in 2012

American Diabetes Association

https://pubmed.ncbi.nlm.nih.gov/25274026/

Monounsaturated fatty acids, olive oil and health status: a systematic review and meta-analysis of cohort studies

Lukas Schwingshackl et al.

https://pubmed.ncbi.nlm.nih.gov/24860193/

Dietary omega-3 fatty acids aid in the modulation of inflammation and metabolic health

Angela M Zivkovic et al.

https://pubmed.ncbi.nlm.nih.gov/18541602/

n-3 Fatty acids and cardiovascular disease: mechanisms underlying beneficial effects

Un Ju Jung et al.

https://pubmed.ncbi.nlm.nih.gov/29897866/

Primary Prevention of Cardiovascular Disease with a Mediterranean Diet Supplemented with Extra-Virgin Olive Oil or Nuts

Ramón Estruch et al.

https://www.ncbi.nlm.nih.gov/pmc/articles/PMC5376310/

Fruit and vegetable intake and the risk of overall cancer in Japanese: A pooled analysis of population-based cohort studies

Ribeka Takachi et al

https://www.ncbi.nlm.nih.gov/books/NBK541064/

Biochemistry, Antioxidants

William L. Stone et al.

Chapter Three - Telomeres

(1)   https://pubmed.ncbi.nlm.nih.gov/21851179/

Rejuvenation Res. 2011 Aug;14(4):457-61.

doi: 10.1089/rej.2011.1237. Personal profile: interview with Bill Andrews, Ph.D.

Bill Andrews PMID: 21851179 DOI: 10.1089/rej.2011.1237

(2)   The researchers of the study are from the Singapore-based biotech company Gero, Roswell Park Comprehensive Cancer Center in Buffalo, New York, and the Kurchatov Institute in Moscow.

(3)   https://www.nature.com/articles/ncomms5172

Chronic inflammation induces telomere dysfunction and accelerates ageing in mice.

1, 2014, Nature Communications, Vol. 5, pp. 4172-4172.

Jurk, Diana, et al.

(4)   https://pubmed.ncbi.nlm.nih.gov/22500274/

National Library of Medicine

Aging and Disease, Vol. 3, pp. 130-140.

Exercise, inflammation and aging.

Woods, Jeffrey A., et al. 1, 2012

(5)   https://pubmed.ncbi.nlm.nih.gov/16136653/

National Library of Medicine

Nature Reviews Genetics, Vol. 6, pp. 611-622.

Telomeres and human disease: ageing, cancer and beyond.

Blasco, Maria A. 8, 2005,

(6) https://www.sciencedirect.com/science/article/abs/pii/S0952327818300747
Science Direct
Omega-6 fatty acids and inflammation
Jacqueline K. Innes, et al.

(7) https://pubmed.ncbi.nlm.nih.gov/19022225/
Russo GL. Dietary n-6 and n-3 polyunsaturated fatty acids: from biochemistry to clinical implications in cardiovascular prevention. Biochem Pharmacol. 2009 Mar 15;77(6):937-46. doi: 10.1016/j.bcp.2008.10.020. Epub 2008 Oct 28. PMID: 19022225

(2) https://www.arthritis.org/health-wellness/healthy-living/nutrition/foods-to-limit/8-food-ingredients-that-can-cause-inflammation
Arthritis Foundation
8 Food Ingredients that can cause inflammation.

(3) https://www.ncbi.nlm.nih.gov/pmc/articles/PMC4808858/
An Increase in the omega-6/omega-3 Fatty Acid Ratio Increases the Risk for Obesity
Artemis P. Simopoulos

(4) https://www.arthritis.org/health-wellness/about-arthritis/understanding-arthritis/fat-and-arthritis
How Fat can worsen arthritis
Andrea Kane

(5) https://easyhealthoptions.com/this-group-of-foods-shortens-your-telomeres-and-triggers-aging/
This group of foods shortens your telomeres and triggers aging
Food Additives – Health News
Healthy Ageing – Dr. DRIA SCHMEDTHORST

(6) https://www.livescience.com/38477-omega3-superstars.html
Live Science
Understanding the Power of omega-3s (Op-Ed)
By Katherine Tallmadge

(7) https://www.ncbi.nlm.nih.gov/pmc/articles/PMC4808858/
An Increase in the omega-6/omega-3 Fatty Acid Ratio Increases the Risk for Obesity
Artemis P. Simopoulos

(8) https ://www.sciencedaily.com/releases/2011/03/110324153712.htm
Eskimo study suggests high consumption of omega-3s in fish-rich diet reduces obesity-related disease risk
Fred Hutchinson Cancer Research Center

(9) https://www.healthline.com/nutrition/anti-inflammatory-diet-101#causes
Anti-Inflammatory Diet 101: How to Reduce Inflammation Naturally

By Franziska Spritzler

(10) https://pubmed.ncbi.nlm.nih.gov/19022225/

Russo GL. Dietary n-6 and n-3 polyunsaturated fatty acids: from biochemistry to clinical implications in cardiovascular prevention. Biochem Pharmacol. 2009 Mar 15;77(6):937-46. Doi: 10.1016/j.bcp.2008.10.020. Epub 2008 Oct 28. PMID: 19022225.

(11) https://www.jacc.org/doi/full/10.1016/j.jacc.2006.04.026

Journal of the American College of Cardiology

AHA/ACC Guidelines for Secondary Prevention for Patients With Coronary and Other Atherosclerotic Vascular Disease: 2006 Update: Endorsed by the National Heart, Lung, and Blood Institute

https://www.nutritionadvance.com/omega-6-to-omega-3-ratio/#:~:text=According%20 to%20some%20researchers%2C%20humans%20evolved%20on%20a,much%20of%20 this%20change%20is%20how%20humans%20eat.

Nutrition Advance

The omega-6 to omega-3 Ratio Has Changed Within Human Diets – But Does It Matter?

(12) https://www.healthline.com/nutrition/anti-inflammatory-diet-101#causes

Anti-Inflammatory Diet 101: How to Reduce Inflammation Naturally

By Franziska Spritzler

(13) https://www.news-medical.net/news/20200831/Eating-ultraprocessed-food-shortens-your-telomeres.aspx#

News – Medical & Life Sciences

Eating ultraprocessed food shortens your telomeres

By Dr. Ananya Mandal, MD

(14) https://pubmed.ncbi.nlm.nih.gov/23468462/

Natl Cancer Inst

Short telomere length, cancer survival, and cancer risk in 47102 individuals

Maren Weischer et al.

(15) https://www.ncbi.nlm.nih.gov/pmc/articles/PMC3370421/

Telomeres, lifestyle, cancer, and aging

Shammas MA. Telomeres, lifestyle, cancer, and aging. Curr Opin Clin Nutr Metab Care. 2011 Jan;14(1):28-34. Doi: 10.1097/MCO.0b013e32834121b1. PMID: 21102320; PMCID: PMC3370421.

(16) https://www.ncbi.nlm.nih.gov/pmc/articles/PMC6316700/Physical Activity and Nutrition: Two Promising Strategies for Telomere Maintenance?

(17) https://medicalxpress.com/news/2016-02-differences-non-organic-meat.html

New study finds clear differences between organic and non-organic milk and meat

by Newcastle University

(18) https://agelessinvesting.com/how-to-lengthen-telomeres/

How To Lengthen Telomeres Naturally In 2023 (7 Remedies)

By Jeremy Mortis

(19) https://www.researchgate.net/publication/227712902_High-intensity_interval_training_and_hypertension_Maximizing_the_benefits_of_exercise#:~:text=intensity%20interval%20training%20%28HIT%29%2C%20which%20consists%20of%20several,high%20familial%20risk%20for%20hypertension%20subjects.%20This%20compelling

American journal of cardiovascular disease, Vol. 2, pp. 102-110.

High-intensity interval training and hypertension: maximizing the benefits of exercise?

Ciolac, Emmanuel Gomes

(20) https://www.researchgate.net/publication/325134827_The_effect_of_high_intensity_interval_training_on_telomere_length_and_telomerase_activity_in_non-athlete_young_men

Journal of Basic Research in Medical Sciences 5(2):1-7

The effect of high intensity interval training on telomere length and telomerase activity in non-athlete young men

Saeedreza Noorimofrad et al.

(21) https://alzheimersprevention.org/research/kirtan-kriya-yoga-exercise/

Alzheimer's Research & Prevention Foundation

Practice the 12-minute Yoga Meditation Exercise

Kirtan Yoga exercise

(22) https://www.bbc.com/future/article/20140701-can-meditation-delay-ageing

BBC - Future

Can meditation help prevent the effects of ageing?

Can meditation really slow down the effects of age? One Nobel Prize-winner is finding the scientific in the spiritual.

Jo Marchant.

(23) https://ncbi.nlm.nih.gov/pmc/articles/PMC3057175/

Annals of the New York Academy of Sciences, Vol. 1172, pp. 34-53

Can meditation slow rate of cellular aging? Cognitive stress, mindfulness, and telomeres

Epel, Elissa S., et al.

(24) https://www.nad.com/news/telomere-restoration-therapy

NAD + Ageing Science

Longevity

Scientists Prolong Mouse Lifespan by Extending Telomeres

Daniel R. Miranda, PhD.

(25) https://www.tasciences.com/what-is-ta-65.html

The science of Telomerase Activation

Chapter Four – Earthing

(1) https://ncbi.nlm.nih.gov/pmc/articles/PMC3265077/

Earthing: Health Implications of Reconnecting the Human Body to the Earth's Surface Electrons

This paper reviews the earthing research and the potential of earthing as a simple and easily accessed global modality of significant clinical importance.

(2) https://www.news.com.au/lifestyle/health/barefoot-for-better-health/news-story/b0e9805bbf390d6fc1f5c2db0865c951

Why healthy people are 'earthing'

It sounds hippy, but planting your bare feet on the earth is actually good for your health. Here's why.

Libby Hakim

(3) https://www.ncbi.nlm.nih.gov/pmc/articles/PMC3265077/

Chevalier, G., Sinatra, S. T., Oschman, J. L., Sokal, K., & Sokal, P. (2012, January 12). Earthing: Health Implications of Reconnecting the Human Body to the Earth's Surface Electrons. Retrieved April 12, 2018, from

(4) https://u.osu.edu/vanzandt/2018/04/18/body-earthing/

Body-Earthing

April 18, 2018 at 12:23pm by van-zandt.2

By Georgia Kinch

https://pubmed.ncbi.nlm.nih.gov/15650465/

The biologic effects of grounding the human body during sleep as measured by cortisol levels and subjective reporting of sleep, pain, and stress. Maurice Ghaly, Dale Teplitz

(5) https://www.scirp.org/reference/ReferencesPapers.aspx?ReferenceID=1333062

Grounding the Human Body Improves Facial Blood Flow Regulation: Results of a Randomized, Placebo Controlled Pilot Study

(6) https://www.huffpost.com/entry/the-healing-benefits-of-grounding-the-human-body_b_592c585be4b07d848fdc058a

The Huffington Post the-healing-benefits-of-grounding-the-human-body_Deepak Chopra

(7) https://townsendletter.com/May2010/earthing0510.html

Earthing: The Most Important Health Discovery Ever?
by Martin Zucker

(8) https://www.goodreads.com/author/list/2085.Martin_Zucker

Earthing: The Most Important Health Discovery Ever?
by Clinton Ober, Stephen T. Sinatra (Goodreads Author), Martin Zucker

(9) https://pubmed.ncbi.nlm.nih.gov/18047442/

Can electrons act as antioxidants? A review and commentary

James L Oschman et al\

(10)   https://pubmed.ncbi.nlm.nih.gov/30982019/
Grounding Patients With Hypertension Improves Blood Pressure: A Case History Series Study

(11)   https://www.goodreads.com/book/show/277641.The_Body_Electric
The Body Electric: Electromagnetism and the Foundation of Life
Robert O Becker M.D.

(12)   https://ncbi.nlm.nih.gov/pmc/articles/PMC2265901/
Immunosenescence: emerging challenges for an ageing population
Danielle Aw

(13)   https ://betterearthing.com.au/earthing-benefits
Products supplier

Chapter Five -The Miracle of Brain Rejuvenation

(1)   https://brainmd.com/dr-daniel-amen
Brain MD – Dr. Daniel Amen's website
https://www.youtube.com/watch?v=MLKj1puoWCg
Dr. Amen – TED presentation

(2)   https://www.livescience.com/burn-calories-brain.html
Live Science
How Many Calories Can the Brain Burn by Thinking?
News
By Emma Bryce

(3)   https://www.health.harvard.edu/blog/nutritional-psychiatry-your-brain-on-food-201511168626
HARVARD HEALTH BLOG
Nutritional psychiatry: Your brain on food
September 18, 2022
By Eva Selhub MD

(4)   https://www.creativityatwork.com/dr-amen-seven-simple-brain-promoting-nutrition-tips/
Seven Simple Brain-Promoting Nutritional Tips
Dr. Amen

(5)   https://www.healthline.com/nutrition/good-carbs-bad-carbs#TOC_TITLE_HDR_3
Healthline
Carbohydrates: Whole vs. Refined — Here's the Difference
Kris Gunnars, BSc — Updated on February 2, 2023

(6)   https://www.goodreads.com/book/show/306368.Sugar_Blues
Sugar Blues by William Duffy

(7)   https://www.dementia.news/2019-05-10-alzheimers-changes-the-brain-years-before-symptoms-begin.html
Alarming study finds that Alzheimer's impairs the brain by 30 years or more BEFORE symptoms get diagnosed
05/10/2019 / By Edsel Cook

(8)   https://pubmed.ncbi.nlm.nih.gov/29024348/
Obesity and Alzheimer's disease: a link between body weight and cognitive function in old age

(9)   https://pubmed.ncbi.nlm.nih.gov/29024348/
Obesity as a risk factor for Alzheimer's disease: weighing the evidence.

(10)   https://www.healthline.com/health-news/how-obesity-may-be-linked-to-alzheimers-disease
Healthline
How Obesity May Be Linked to Alzheimer's Disease
By Eileen Bailey on January 31, 2023 — Fact checked by Dana K. Cassell

(11)   https://www.livescience.com/10582-obese-people-severe-brain-degeneration.html
Obese People Have 'Severe Brain Degeneration'
By Live Science Staff
published August 25, 2009

(12)   https://pubmed.ncbi.nlm.nih.gov/23107018/
Obesity is associated with a lower resting oxygen saturation in the ambulatory elderly: results from the cardiovascular health study.

(13)   https://blackdoctor.org/3-ways-to-get-more-oxygen-to-the-brain/
3 ways to get more oxygen to the brain

(14)   http://www.nacd.org/my-brain-needs-oxygen-what-can-i-do/
My brain needs more oxygen – what can I do?   By Steve Riggs

(15)   https://www.yogajournal.com/poses/cobra-pose-2/
Yoga journal – Cobra pose

(16)   https://www.creativityatwork.com/amen-7-ways-to-optimize-your-brain-your-life/
7 ways to optimize your brain – your life
Dr. Amen

(17)   https://www.amenclinics.com/blog/11-ways-youre-lowering-blood-flow-to-your-brain-and-why-you-should-care/
11 Ways You're Lowering Blood Flow to Your Brain (and Why You Should Care)
February 27, 2020
Dr. Amen

(18)   https://en.wikipedia.org/wiki/Michael_Colgan_(nutritionist) (Who is Michael Colgan?)

(19)   https://transformyourbody4life.blogspot.com/2015/03/dr-michael-colgan-daily-amounts-of.html
Transform your body for life –
Daily amounts of Protein
Dr. Michael Colgan

(20)   Colgan M. Optimum Sports Nutrition. New York. Advanced Research Press. 1993.

Chapter Six – The Brain and Epigenetics –– Mitochondria –– Psychiatry

(1)   https://en.wikipedia.org/wiki/EpigeneticsEpigenetics –– Definitions

(2)   https://www.cdc.gov/genomics/disease/epigenetics.htm
Centres for Disease Control and Prevention
Genomics and Precision Health

(3)   https://www.lindau-nobel.org/epigenetics-how-the-environment-influences-our-genes/
Lindau Nobel Laureate Meetings
Pub. 8May 2015 by Stephanie Hanel.

(4)   https://www.europeanscientist.com/en/research/epigenetics-and-iq-a-new-study-uncovers-one-of-the-mechanisms-behind-environmentally-induced-effects-on-cognitive-performance/
Epigenetics and IQ: the mechanism behind environmentally-induced effects on cognitive performance
Pub. Siobhán Dunphy –– 24.09.2018

(5)   https://www.encyclopedie-environnement.org/en/health/epigenetics-how-the-environment-influences-our-genes/
Encyclopedia of the environment
Epigenetics: How the environment influences our genes
09-06-2021
DROUET Emmanuel, Doctor of Pharmacy, Professor at the Université Grenoble-Alpes, Professor at Institut de biologie structurale UMR 5075 CNRS UGA CEA, Grenoble.

(6)   https://sciencing.com/bee-become-queen-bee-5200755.html
Updated November 05, 2018
By Claire Gillespie

(7)   Epigenetics integration of environmental and genomic signals in honeybees: the critical interplay of nutritional, brain and reproductive networks
Ryszard Maleszka

(8)   https://neurosciencenews.com/celiac-disease-brain-15829/
Neuroscience News –– University of Sheffield –– March 1, 2020

(9)   https://neurosciencenews.com/celiac-disease-brain-15829
        "Cognitive Deficit and White Matter Changes in Persons with Celiac Disease: a Population-Based Study". Iain Croall et al.
        Gastroenterology doi :10.1053/j.gastro.2020.02.028.

(10)   https ://www.amazon.com/Immortality-Edge-Realize-Telomeres-Healthier/dp/1630260193
        The Immortality Edge: Realize the Secrets of Your Telomeres for a Longer, Healthier Life
        Dr. Dave Woynarowski

(11)   https://thelongevityedge.com/ta65/accelerants-of-aging/
        The Longevity Edge – Accelerants of ageing.
        Dr. Dave Woynarowski

(12)   https://www.amazon.com/Anti-Inflammation-Zone-Reversing-Epidemic-Destroying/dp/0060834145
        The Anti-Inflammation Zone: Reversing the Silent Epidemic That's Destroying Our Health (The Zone)
        Paperback – December 13, 2005
        Dr. Barry Sears

(13)   https://www.mitoq.com/journal/what-are-free-radicals
        MitoQ is a world-first, mitochondria-rejuvenating CoQ10 antioxidant.
        REVIEWED BY
        Brendon Woodhead PhD., MSc., BSc.

(14)   https://pubmed.ncbi.nlm.nih.gov/12666097/
        Bioenergetic approaches for neuroprotection in Parkinson's disease
        M Flint Beal
        Ann Neurol. 2003;53 Suppl 3:S39-47; discussion S47-8. Doi: 10.1002/ana.10479.

(15)   https://www.sciencedirect.com/topics/nursing-and-health-professions/caloric-restriction
        Nutrition in the Second Half of Life
        R. Chernoff, in Reference Module in Biomedical Sciences, 2014

(16)   https:// en.wikipedia.org/wiki/Terry_Wahls (Who is Terry Wahl)

(17)   https://www.mswellnessroute.com/what-is-the-wahls-protocol/
        MS Wellness Route
        The Wahl's Protocole – Dr. Wahls

(18)   https://valentinosnaturals.com/kale-brain-benefits/
        Kale Brain Benefits: Is Kale Good for Your Brain?
        Valentino M.

(19)   https://www.healthline.com/nutrition/organ-meats
        Are Organ Meats Healthy
        Daisy Coyle,

(20)   Calton JB. Prevalence of micronutrient deficiency in popular diet plans. J Int Soc Sports
        Nutr. 2010;7:24.

(21) https://theenergyblueprint.com/wp-content/uploads/2022/04/The-Top-Science-Backed-Supplements-To-Boost-Your-Energy-Brain-Performance-And-Mood-Resilience.pdf
The Energy Blueprint – The Top Science Based Supplements to Boost You Energy Brain Performance and Mood Resilience.

(22) https://drewramseymd.com/
Founder, Brain Food Clinic in New York City
Creator, Nutritional Psychiatry for Healthcare Professionals

(23) Fifty Shades of Kale
Authors: Dr. Drew Ramsey and Jennifer Iserloh
ISBN: 9780062272881
ISBN 10: 0062272888
Imprint: HarperCollins US

(24) https://pubmed.ncbi.nlm.nih.gov/30117106/
National Library of Medicine
Epub 2018 Aug 17.
Brain-Derived Neurotrophic Factor in Brain Disorders: Focus on Neuroinflammation
Bruno Lima Giacobbo

(25) https://learn.drewramseymd.com/nutritional-psychiatry-reg-eg/
How Adding Nutritional Psychiatry To My Practice Empowers My Patients To Get Better & STAY Better by Dr. Drew Ramsay

(26) https://drewramseymd.com/brain-food-nutrition/9-mechanisms-of-nutritional-psychiatry/
9 Mechanisms of Nutritional Psychiatry
https://drewramseymd.com/brain-food-nutrition/foods-to-improve-anxiety/
Foods to Improve Anxiety

(27) https://drewramseymd.com/brain-food-nutrition/7-foods-i-prescribe-most-often-for-depression/
7 Foods I Prescribe Most Often for Depression

(28) https://theenergyblueprint.com/

(29) https://the energyblueprint.com/wp-content/uploads/2022/04/The-Top-Science-Backed-Supplements-To-Boost-Your-Energy-Brain-Performance-And-Mood-Resilience.pdf
The Energy Blueprint – The Top Science Based Supplements to Boost You Energy Brain Performance and Mood Resilience.

Chapter Seven - Stem Cells support & Superfoods --- The three treasures for Longevity.

(1) https://www.fitneass.com/how-to-restore-jing-energy/?amp
How to restore Jing Energy

(2) https://www.superfoodevolution.com/chinese-herbs.html#
Superfoods Evolution – Chines Herbs – Superior Tonics

(3)   https://www.healthline.com/health/qi-deficiency#symptoms
        Healthline.com
        Qi deficiency symptoms

(4)   https://stemcells.nih.gov/info/basics/stc-basics/
        National Health Institute
        Stem Cells basics

(5)   http://www.stemcellnutrition.net/
        Mark Anderson

(6)   "Stem Cells – the Building Blocks of the Body"
        Christian Drapeau MSc.

(7)   https://www.ncbi.nlm.nih.gov/pmc/articles/PMC4684114/
        Medicinal Mushrooms: Ancient Remedies Meet Modern Science
        Paul Stamets

(8)   https://www.ncbi.nlm.nih.gov/pmc/articles/PMC4684115/
        Immune Modulation From Five Major Mushrooms: Application to Integrative Oncology
        Alena G. Guggenheim et al.

(9)   https ://pubmed.ncbi.nlm.nih.gov/22593926/
        Ganoderma lucidum (Lingzhi or Reishi): A Medicinal Mushroom
        Sissi Wachtel-Galor et al
        In: Herbal Medicine: Biomolecular and Clinical Aspects. 2nd edition. Boca Raton (FL): CRC
        Press/Taylor & Francis; 2011. Chapter 9.

(10)   https://pubmed.ncbi.nlm.nih.gov/14756912/
        Ganoderma lucidum ("Lingzhi"), a Chinese medicinal mushroom: biomarker responses in a
        controlled human supplementation study.
        Sissi Wachtel-Galor et al

(11)   https://scholar.nycu.edu.tw/en/publications/ganoderma-lucidum-polysaccharides-in-
        human-monocytic-leukemia-cel
        Ganoderma lucidum polysaccharides in human monocytic leukemia cells: from gene
        expression to network construction.
        Cheng KC, Huang HC, Chen JH, et al.

(12)   https ://experts.umn.edu/en/publications/ganoderma-lucidum-extracts-inhibited-leukemia-
        wehi-3-cells-in-bal
        Ganoderma lucidum extracts inhibited leukemia WEHI-3 cells in BALB/c mice and promoted
        an immune response in vivo
        Chang YH, Yang JS, Yang JL, et al..

(13)   https ://www.medicalnewstoday.com/articles/324710
        Does eating mushrooms protect brain health?
        By Maria Cohut, Ph.D. on March 15, 2019 — Fact checked by Jasmin Collier

(14)   https://www.superfeast.com.au/products/lions-mane-mushroom-powdered-extract
        Lions Mane Mushroom

209

(15) https ://www.verywellfit.com/lion-s-mane-nutrition-facts-and-health-benefits-5185393
The Health Benefits of Lion's Mane
Brain Health, Anti-Cancer, Anti-Diabetic   By Malia Frey

(16) https://pubmed.ncbi.nlm.nih.gov/18844328/
Improving effects of the mushroom Yamabushitake (Hericium erinaceus) on mild cognitive impairment: a double-blind placebo-controlled clinical trial.
Mori K, Inatomi S, Ouchi K, Azumi Y, Tuchida T.
Phytother Res. 2009;23(3):367-72. Doi:10.1002/ptr.2634

(17) https://www.dl.begellhouse.com/
journals/708ae68d64b17c52,034eeb045436a171,750a15ad12ae25e9.html
International Journal of Medicinal Mushrooms
Editor-in-Chief: Solomon P. Wasser
Volume 15, 2013 Issue 6

(18) https://www.medicalnewstoday.com/articles/improving-memory-lions-mane-mushrooms-may-double-neuron-growth
Improving memory: Lion's mane mushrooms may double neuron growth
By Hannah Flynn on February 17, 2023 — Fact checked by Alexandra Sanfins, Ph.D.

(19) https://www.stemcellsnutrition.net/afa-super-blue-green-algae/
Benefits Of Consuming AFA Blue-Green Algae

(20) www.superfoodevolution.com/marine-phytoplankton.html
Marine Phytoplankton Benefits, A Nutrient Dense Microalgae Supplement

(21) https://www.youtube.com/watch?v=5Leqq3gQgdQ&t=11s
Marine Phytoplankton, A Nutrient Dense Microalgae

(22) https ://pubmed.ncbi.nlm.nih.gov/33572056/
Edible Microalgae and Their Bioactive Compounds in the Prevention and Treatment of Metabolic Alterations.
Ramos-Romero S

(23) https://pubmed.ncbi.nlm.nih.gov/28656633/
The roles of B vitamins in phytoplankton nutrition: new perspectives and prospects
Katherine E Helliwell

(24) https://pubmed.ncbi.nlm.nih.gov/25954194/
Long-chain omega-3 fatty acids and the brain: a review of the independent and shared effects of EPA, DPA and DHA
Simon C Dyall

(25) https://pubmed.ncbi.nlm.nih.gov/20329590/
Essential fatty acids and human brain:
Chia-Yu Chang

(26) https://www.youtube.com/watch?v=3dw_LWQcwEQ
Blue Green Algae, A Superfood for the Brain and More

(27) https://au.activationproducts.com/products/oceans-alive
OCEANS ALIVE -– Activation Products Australia

(28) https://www.valterlongo.com/

(29) https://en.wikipedia.org/wiki/Valter_Longo (Who is Valter Longo)

(30) The Longevity Diet by Professor Valter Longo
Publisher PENGUIN LIFE AUS
Publication date 22 January 2018
ISBN-13 978-0143788379

(31) https://www.valterlongo.com/how-fasting-resets-your-biology-and-helps-you-live-longer-valter-longo-ph-d-with-dave-asprey/
How Fasting Resets Your Biology and Helps You Live Longer – Valter Longo, Ph.D., with Dave Asprey

Chapter Eight - Stress and Meditation

(1) https://pubmed.ncbi.nlm.nih.gov/18190880/
Stress as a trigger of autoimmune disease
Ljudmila Stojanovich

(2) https://draxe.com/health/reduce-stress-to-beat-autoimmune/?utm_source=curated&utm_medium=email&utm_campaign=20230405_curated_freeshipping-site
7 Ways to Reduce Stress to Beat Autoimmune
By Palmer Kippola

(3) https://www.huffpost.com/entry/keeping-your-prefrontal-c_b_679290
Keeping Your Prefrontal Cortex Online: Neuroplasticity, Stress and Meditation
By Jeanne Ball -– https://www.huffpost.com/author/jeanne-ball

(4) https://journals.plos.org/plosone/article?id=10.1371/journal.pone.0140212
Relaxation Response and Resiliency Training and Its Effect on Healthcare Resource Utilization
James E. Stahl et al.

(5) https ://www.sciencedaily.com/releases/2008/09/080902075211.htm
Loss Of Sleep, Even For A Single Night, Increases Inflammation In The Body
Date: September 4, 2008
Source: Elsevier

(6) https://pubmed.ncbi.nlm.nih.gov/24380741/
Breathing at a rate of 5.5 breaths per minute with equal inhalation-to-exhalation ratio increases heart rate variability
I M Lin et al

(7)   https://pubmed.ncbi.nlm.nih.gov/25599350/
Sedentary time and its association with risk for disease incidence, mortality, and hospitalization in adults: a systematic review and meta-analysis
Aviroop Biswas et al

(8)   https://www.sciencedirect.com/science/article/abs/pii/S1568997212001322?via%3Dihub
Exercise as a therapeutic tool to counteract inflammation and clinical symptoms in autoimmune rheumatic diseases
Luiz Augusto Perandini et al

(9)   https://www.businessinsider.com/scientific-benefits-of-nature-outdoors-2016-4
11 scientific reasons you should be spending more time outside
Lauren F Friedman and Kevin Loria,
Tech Insider   Apr 23, 2016

(10)   https://www.outsideonline.com/health/wellness/take-two-hours-pine-forest-and-call-me-morning/?scope=anon
Take Two Hours of Pine Forest and Call Me in the Morning
Florence Williams

(11)   https://www.self.com/story/sunlight-benefits
6 Reasons You Need More Sun, According To Science
How to get the proven benefits of sunlight—safely.
By Elizabeth Millard, C.P.T., R.Y.T. – April 12, 2016

(12)   https://www.hopkinsmedicine.org/health/wellness-and-prevention/forgiveness-your-health-depends-on-it
Forgiveness: Your Health Depends on It
Karen Swartz, M.D., director of the Mood Disorders Adult Consultation Clinic at The Johns Hopkins Hospital.

(13)   https://www.sciencedirect.com/science/article/abs/pii/S0889159113005370?via%3Dihub
Brain, Behavior, and Immunity
Volume 37, March 2014, Pages 109-114
Self-compassion as a predictor of interleukin-6 response to acute psychosocial stress
Juliana G. Breines et al.

(14)   https://www.forbes.com/health/mind/benefits-of-meditation/
10 Science-Backed Benefits Of Meditation
By Zameena Mejia

(15)   https://www.healthline.com/nutrition/12-benefits-of-meditation
12 Science-Based Benefits of Meditation
Medically reviewed by Marney A. White, PhD, MS, Psychology — By Matthew Thorpe, MD, PhD and Rachael Ajmera, MS, RD — Updated on October 27, 2020

(16) https://www.huffpost.com/entry/meditation-tips_b_3791316
3 Ways Meditation Helps You Deal With Adversity
Meditation can be a tool that anchors us to the inner side of life, the side that is beyond the ups and downs of change, that is eternal, timeless and untouched.
Jeanne Ball (35-Year Teacher of the Transcendental Meditation technique)

(17) https://hbr.org/2015/12/why-google-target-and-general-mills-are-investing-in-mindfulness
Why Google, Target, and General Mills Are Investing in Mindfulness
by Kimberly Schaufenbuel

(18) https://www.theguardian.com/sustainable-business/google-meditation-mindfulness-technology
Google's head of mindfulness: 'goodness is good for business'
Chade-Meng Tan, the search engine giant's Jolly Good Fellow, on meditation, acceptance and the power of positive business

(19) https://rpl.hds.harvard.edu/religion-context/case-studies/technology/mindfulness-silicon-valley
Mindfulness in Silicon Valley
Buddhism Case Study – Technology I2019

(20) https://pubmed.ncbi.nlm.nih.gov/22473771/
Diversity matters: the importance of comparative studies and the potential for synergy between neuroscience and evolutionary biology
Bruce A Carlson

(21) https://pubmed.ncbi.nlm.nih.gov/26784917/
Mindfulness meditation practice and executive functioning: Breaking down the benefit
Sara N Gallant

(22) https ://www.sciencedirect.com/science/article/abs/pii/S0166432815302278
Impact of short-term meditation and expectation on executive brain functions
Martin Prätzlich

(23) https://chopra.com/articles/how-meditation-helps-your-immune-system-do-its-job
How Meditation Helps Your Immune System Do its Job
Deepak Chopra

(24) https://www.forbes.com/sites/forbescoachescouncil/2019/11/26/cultivating-employee-engagement-with-emotional-connection/?sh=386a38fa2eba
Cultivating Employee Engagement With Emotional Connection
Louis Carter

(25) https ://sps.columbia.edu/news/how-meditation-can-help-you-focus#:
How Meditation Can Help You Focus

(26) https://pubmed.ncbi.nlm.nih.gov/24626068/
Effect of transcendental meditation on employee stress, depression, and burnout: a randomized controlled study by Charles Elder et al

(27) https://pubmed.ncbi.nlm.nih.gov/36121655/
Efficacy of Transcendental Meditation to Reduce Stress Among Health Care Workers: A Randomized Clinical Trial
Sangeeta P Joshi et al

(28) https ://www.tm.org/research-on-meditation
More than 380 peer-reviewed research studies on the TM technique have been published in over 160 scientific journals. These studies were conducted at many US and international universities and research centers, including Harvard Medical School, Stanford Medical School, Yale Medical School, and UCLA Medical School.

(29) https://www.huffpost.com/entry/meditation-at-work_n_55ba4de4e4b0af35367a7e7b
Transcendental Meditation Is Going Corporate. Here's Why That's A Good Thing.
These skills boost employee health and the bottom line.
By Alena Hall

(30) Psycho-Cybernetics (Updated and Expanded)
By: Maxwell Maltz
Published: 15th November 2022
ISBN: 9781800812918

(31) Harvard Business Review
How Meditation Benefits CEOs
Emma Seppälä

(32) https ://www.everydayhealth.com/meditation/highly-successful-ceos-celebrities-who-practice-meditation/
8 Highly Successful CEOs and Celebrities Who Practice Meditation

(33) https://daveasprey.com/hack-your-stress-and-sex-with-these-7-adaptogens/
12 Best Adaptogens to Feel Less Stressed, Get Laser Focused and More

(34) http://www.ncbi.nlm.nih.gov/pubmed/23439798
A prospective, randomized double-blind, placebo-controlled study of safety and efficacy of a high-concentration full-spectrum extract of ashwagandha root in reducing stress and anxiety in adults
K Chandrasekhar et al

(35) http ://www.ncbi.nlm.nih.gov/pubmed/19718255
Naturopathic care for anxiety: a randomized controlled trial ISRCTN78958974
Kieran Cooley et al

(36) http ://www.ncbi.nlm.nih.gov/pubmed/22208270
Computational evidence to inhibition of human acetyl cholinesterase by withanolide a for Alzheimer treatment
Abhinav Grover et al

(37)   http://www.ncbi.nlm.nih.gov/pubmed/12410544
Antistress effects of bacosides of Bacopa monnieri: modulation of Hsp70 expression, superoxide dismutase and cytochrome P450 activity in rat brain
D Kar Chowdhuri et al

(38)   http://www.ncbi.nlm.nih.gov/pubmed/12957224
Adaptogenic effect of Bacopa Monniera (Brahmi)
Deepak Rai et al

(39)   http://www.ncbi.nlm.nih.gov/pubmed/21619917
Double-blinded randomized controlled trial for immunomodulatory effects of Tulsi (Ocimum sanctum Linn.) leaf extract on healthy volunteers
Shankar Mondal et al

(40)   http://www.ncbi.nlm.nih.gov/pubmed/7275241
Anti-stress activity of Ocimum sanctum Linn
K P Bhargava, N Singh

(41)   http://www.ncbi.nlm.nih.gov/pubmed/19253862
Controlled programmed trial of Ocimum sanctum leaf on generalized anxiety disorders
D Bhattacharyya et al

(42)   https://daveasprey.com/mucuna-pruriens-dopa-bean/
Mucuna Pruriens: Discover the Benefits of this Mood-Boosting Productivity Supplement
Dave Asprey

(43)   https://daveasprey.com/hack-your-stress-and-sex-with-these-7-adaptogens/#ref-list
12 Best Adaptogens to Feel Less Stressed, Get Laser Focused and More
Dave Asprey

(44)   https://pubmed.ncbi.nlm.nih.gov/25364207/
Dopamine mediated antidepressant effect of Mucuna pruriens seeds in various experimental models of depression
Digvijay G Rana et al

Chapter Nine – Ageless SKIN – Youthful Appearance

(1)   https://journals.sagepub.com/doi/10.1177/0963721416683996
Sage Journals
First Impressions From Faces
Leslie A. Zebrowitz

(2)   https://www.statista.com/forecasts/1268473/worldwide-revenue-skin-care-market.
Worldwide Revenue Skin Care Market

(3)   https://pubmed.ncbi.nlm.nih.gov/24527317/
Characteristics of the Aging Skin by Miranda A Farage

(4)   https://pubmed.ncbi.nlm.nih.gov/29692196
         Fighting against Skin Aging: The Way from Bench to Bedside by Shoubing Zhang

(5)   https://www.livescience.com/does-gut-health-affect-skin
         Live Science
         Does gut health affect skin?
         By Anna Gora - Dr. Brooke Jeffy interview

(6)   https://www.researchgate.net/publication/357178028 Microbiome and Human Aging
         Probiotic and Prebiotic Potentials in Longevity Skin Health and Cellular Senescence
         Research Gate
         Microbiome and Human Aging: Probiotic and Prebiotic Potentials in Longevity, Skin Health
         and Cellular Senescence by Jacqueline Boyajian et al

(7)   https://pubmed.ncbi.nlm.nih.gov/25754370/
         The Achilles' heel of senescent cells: from transcriptome to senolytic drugs
         Yi Zhu

(8)   https://pubmed.ncbi.nlm.nih.gov/33262144/
         SASP = senescence-associated secretory phenotype

(9)   https://mayoclinic.pure.elsevier.com/en/publications/senolytic-combination-of-dasatinib-
         and-quercetin-alleviates-intes
         Senolytic Combination of Dasatinib and Quercetin Alleviates Intestinal Senescence and
         Inflammation and Modulates the Gut Microbiome in Aged Mice
         Tatiana Dandolini Saccon, et al

(10)   https://pubmed.ncbi.nlm.nih.gov/29737207/
         Restoring Effects of Natural Anti-Oxidant Quercetin on Cellular Senescent Human Dermal
         Fibroblasts
         Eun-Ju Sohn et al

(11)   https://www.researchgate.net/publication/45148437 Anti-ageing and rejuvenating
         effects of quercetin#:
         Anti-ageing and rejuvenating effects of quercetin
         Niki Chondrogianni et al

(12)   https://pubmed.ncbi.nlm.nih.gov/23494974/
         Skin health promotion effects of natural beta-glucan derived from cereals and
         microorganisms: a review
         Bin Du

(13)   https://pubmed.ncbi.nlm.nih.gov/30196242/
         A critical review on the impacts of β-glucans on gut microbiota and human health
         Muthukumaran Jayachandran

(14)   https://pubmed.ncbi.nlm.nih.gov/29439479/
         Zinc and Skin Disorders
         Youichi Ogawa

(15) https://www.researchgate.net/publication/349523883_Effect_of_Lactobacillus_reuteri_Administration_on_Wrinkle_Formation_and_Type_I_Procollagen_Levels_in_UVB-Exposed_Male_Balbc_Mice_Mus_musculus

Effect of Lactobacillus reuteri Administration on Wrinkle Formation and Type I Procollagen Levels in UVB-Exposed Male Balb/c Mice (Mus musculus)

Ivanna Valentina

(16) https://pubmed.ncbi.nlm.nih.gov/23342023/

Probiotic bacteria induce a 'glow of health'

Tatiana Levkovich et al.

(17) https://pubmed.ncbi.nlm.nih.gov/32802255/

Diet and Dermatology: The Role of a Whole-food, Plant-based Diet in Preventing and Reversing Skin Aging-A Review

Jason Solway et al.

(18) https://pubmed.ncbi.nlm.nih.gov/32802255/

Diet and Dermatology: The Role of a Whole-food, Plant-based Diet in Preventing and Reversing Skin Aging-A Review

The Journal of clinical and aesthetic dermatology

The Roles of Vitamin C in Skin Health. Nutrients

Jason Solway et al

(19) https://pubmed.ncbi.nlm.nih.gov/33494277/

Illuminating the Role of Vitamin A in Skin Innate Immunity and the Skin Microbiome: A Narrative Review by Fritzlaine C Roche et al

(20) https://pubmed.ncbi.nlm.nih.gov/20085665/

Association of dietary fat, vegetables and antioxidant micronutrients with skin ageing in Japanese women

Chisato Nagata et al.

Other reference:

https://www.fightaging.org/archives/2020/12/a-review-of-senolytics-biotech-companies/

A review of Senolytics Biotech Companies

Chapter Ten - Sleep: Your secret superpower

(1) https://www.ninds.nih.gov/health-information/public-education/brain-basics/brain-basics-understanding-sleep

National Institute of Neurological Disorders and Strokes (NINDS). (2019, August 13). Brain basics: Understanding Sleep., Retrieved October 5, 2020

(2) https://www.ncbi.nlm.nih.gov/books/NBK526132/

Physiology, Sleep Stages. StatPearls Publishing.

Patel, A. K., et al. (2020, April)

(3) http://healthysleep.med.harvard.edu/healthy/science/what/sleep-patterns-rem-nrem
Division of Sleep Medicine at Harvard Medical School. (2007, December 18). Natural Patterns of Sleep.

(4) https://www.sleepfoundation.org/how-sleep-works#references-78178
Sleep foundation – How sleep works

(5) https://pubmed.ncbi.nih.gov/27212237/
Sleep Drive Is Encoded by Neural Plastic Changes in a Dedicated Circuit. Cell, 165(6), 1347–1360. By Liu, S., Liu, et al. (2016).

(6) https://pubmed.ncbi.nlm.nih.gov/21172606/
Sleep state switching. Neuron, 68(6), 1023–1042.
Saper, et al. (2010).

(7) https://pubmed.ncbi.nlm.nih.gov/31256784/
Circadian Neurobiology and the Physiologic Regulation of Sleep and Wakefulness. Neurologic clinics, 37(3), 475–486.
Schwartz, W. J., & Klerman, E. B. (2019).

(8) https://pubmed.ncbi.nlm.nih.gov/25861266/
National Library of Medicine, The National Center for Biotechnology Information
The impact of sleep and circadian disturbance on hormones and metabolism. International journal of endocrinology, 2015, 591729
Kim, T. W., Jeong, J. H., & Hong, S. C. (2015).

(9) https://news.harvard.edu/gazette/story/2020/06/study-reveals-guts-role-in-causing-death-by-sleep-deprivation/
Harvard Education Gazette-
Study reveals gut's role in causing death by sleep deprivation.

(10) https://www.ncbi.nlm.nih.gov/pubmed/20469800https://www.ncbi.nlm.nih.gov/pubmed/20469800
Sleep duration and all-cause mortality: a systematic review and meta-analysis of prospective studies. Sleep, 33(5), 585–592
Cappuccio, F. P., et al. (2010).

(11) https://intuition-physician.com/insomnia-skyrockets-your-risk-depression-anxiety/
Missing Just One Hour Of Sleep Skyrockets Your Risk Of Depression, Anxiety
Laura Koniver, MD - May 1, 2017

(12) Associations between sleep disturbances, mental health outcomes and burnout in firefighters, and the mediating role of sleep during overnight work: A cross-sectional study. J Sleep Res. 2019;28(6):e12869.
Wolkow AP, et al.

(13)   Insufficient sleep predicts clinical burnout. J Occup Health Psychol. 2012;17(2):175–83.
        Söderström M, et al.

(14)   https://www.sleephealthfoundation.org.au/burnout-and-sleep.html
        Sleep Health Foundation
        Burnout-and-sleep

(15)   Burnout syndrome and depression. In: Understanding Depression: Volume 2
        Clinical Manifestations, Diagnosis and Treatment. 2018. p. 187–202.
        Bianchi R, Schonfeld IS, Laurent E.

(16)   It's not just Time Off : A Framework for Understanding Factors Promoting Recovery From
        Burnout Among Internal Medicine Residents. J Grad Med Educ. 2018;10(1):26–32.
        Abedini NC, et al.

(17)   https://www.headington-institute.org/resource/what-to-do-about-burnout-identifying-your-
        sources/
        The Headington Institute
        What to do about burnout: Identifying your sources.
        Pearlman, L. (2012).

(18)   https://www.headington-institute.org/resource/preventing-burnout/
        The Headington Institute
        Preventing burnout.   By Pearlman, L. (2013).

(19)   The Burnout Fix: Overcome overwhelm, beat busy, and sustain success in the new world of
        work.
        New York: McGraw Hill.
        Jimenez, J. M. (2021).

(20)   BiOptimizers_SleepDeepAndDominate.pdf
        BiOptimizers
        BRIBE – COMPLETE Sleep Chapter
        Chapter 11 – The Biological Optimization Blueprint 2.11.2020

(21)   https://www.youtube.com/watch?v=Us8n8VBQn_c
        Dr. Matthew Walker Matriculated at Nottingham University where he studied neuroscience,
        Matthew earned his Ph.D. in neurophysiology from the Medical Research Council in
        London, subsequently became a Professor of Psychiatry at Harvard Medical School.
        Dr. Matthew Walker is currently a professor of neuroscience and psychology at
        the University of California, Berkeley, where he serves as the founder and director of
        the Center for Human Sleep Science.. As an academic and public intellectual, Walker has
        focused on the impact of sleep on human health.

(22)   https://www.theceomagazine.com/business/health-wellbeing/sleeping-habits-successful-
        people/
        The CEO Magazine
        Business- Well Being – Sleeping habits successful people.

(23) https://www.somabreath.com/scientific-explanation-of-soma-breath/
Soma Breath – Scientific explanation of Soma Breath.

(24) https://solfeggioguide.com/solfeggio-frequency-guide/
Solfeggio frequency guide

(25) Healing Codes For The Biological Apocalypse book (PDF Download Version)
SKU: HC PDF

Other sources

https://thelongevityedge.com/author/drdave/

Scientists discussing the important of sleep.

Alison Divine, PhD, Lecturer in Sport and Exercise Psychology, School of Biomedical Sciences, Sport, and Exercise Sciences, University of Leeds

Christine Parsons, PhD, Interacting Minds Center, Department of Clinical Medicine, Aarhus University

Katherine Young, PhD, King's College London, Silver Cloud Health

Printed in Australia
Ingram Content Group Australia Pty Ltd
AUHW021207031023
384477AU00011B/11